INSPIRATIONAL
LEADERSHIP

First published in 2017 by Libri Publishing ■ Copyright © Chris Edger and Tony Hughes ■ The right of Chris Edger and Tony Hughes to be identified as the authors of this work has been asserted in accordance with the Copyright, Designs and Patents Act, 1988. ■ ISBN 978 1 911450 10 8 ■ All rights reserved. No part of this publication may be reproduced, stored in any retrieval system or transmitted in any form or by any means, electronic, mechanical, photocopying, recording or otherwise, without the prior written permission of the copyright holder for which application should be addressed in the first instance to the publishers. No liability shall be attached to the author, the copyright holder or the publishers for loss or damage of any nature suffered as a result of reliance on the reproduction of any of the contents of this publication or any errors or omissions in its contents. ■ A CIP catalogue record for this book is available from The British Library ■ Design by Helen Taylor ■ Printed in the UK by Hobbs the Printers

Libri Publishing, Brunel House, Volunteer Way, Faringdon, Oxfordshire SN7 7YR

Tel: +44 (0)845 873 3837

www.libripublishing.co.uk

INSPIRATIONAL LEADERSHIP

Mobilising Super-performance through eMOTION

Chris Edger and
Tony Hughes

Foreword by Mike Amos
(founder of Empathica)

LIBRI
PUBLISHING

Foreword

Mike Amos

*Founder of Empathica, Chief Strategy
Officer of Nudge Rewards*

Inspirational Leadership is a brilliant exposition on the art and science of truly exceptional hospitality, retail and service leadership. This book could only be written by a team of seasoned retail and hospitality professionals, people who have dedicated their lives to the study and practice of inspirational leadership. Chris Edger and Tony Hughes have been on a multi-decade journey to uncover the essence of inspirational leadership excellence: a journey which finds its completion one step closer with this book.

Writing the foreword for *Inspirational Leadership* is humbling, for I today find myself on a similar journey, one that has yet to find its final destination. Similar to Chris and Tony, I have spent most of my adult life working to help brands deliver their customer promise through exceptional team efforts.

My journey began when I started working for KFC (then owned by PepsiCo) and it was terrifying. It was like a torrid, youthful love affair, full of the best and worst moments: moments that would change me forever and send me on a more-than-20-year journey, a journey that led me to Tony Hughes, Chris Edger and this fine piece of work.

As an organisation, PepsiCo had mastered several of the competencies outlined in *Inspirational Leadership* and emphasised in its key concept, eMOTION. The company had an intense and exciting culture: one in which intrapreneurialism and empowerment were cornerstones of the operating ethos. It was these cornerstones that made the place so incredible and so incredibly scary. Working there was also like being part of a huge-scale Darwinian experiment where their best and brightest were promoted quickly and expected to sink or swim.

In 1994, I was one of those lucky souls who were learning how to swim. As the youngest area manager in the company, I was in at the deep end as most of my direct reports were significantly older than me and all of them had more experience in field operations. If I was to be successful in my role at PepsiCo, I needed to be at my very best. I certainly would have greatly benefited from a copy of this book!

My initial plan was simple: really understand the performance of my locations, show humility (learn the operations from my team) and build a context for performance improvement. As young success-oriented professionals often do, I initially tried to boil the ocean, focusing on every KPI, visiting the locations and creating visit reports and scores at a dizzying pace. All the while, I was hoping that the numbers would lead my team to improvement or, as Tom Peters (the American management guru) would say: "what gets measured, gets managed." But, I made a huge mistake, I had forgotten the third part of my plan: create a context for performance improvement – or as Chris and Tony might say, "Put the 'e' in the management of your team".

I was reminded about the importance of context and emotion by a dear friend and colleague, Jackie Clark, who one day on the way in to visit a facility said, "Can you at least ask the people how they are doing before you audit or jump into the numbers they need to fix?" It's funny how sometimes the most innocent statements had a way of crystallising my view on a major issue.

At that time, my district was middle of the pack nationally, but her suggestion had started a fire inside me, one that would change me, my team and my market. I realised that the business I was measuring couldn't improve unless the people improved: I needed to change their mindsets, behaviour and capabilities in order to drive the numbers that I held so near and dear to my heart. My focus turned to the context of the business and the *emotional* side of management. Within six months we were first or second in the country in every KPI. We beat our sales budget, achieved nation-leading mystery shopping scores and improved operating margins by 50 per cent. Better yet, we had the most talented team in the country. This left me with the firm belief that people are the most important asset in a business and context is a manager's most important goal: one that emulates the requirements laid out in *Inspirational Leadership*.

Several years went by and I moved through several roles of increasingly challenging assignments ending at the senior vice president level in one of Canada's largest companies. The recession hit in 2001 and I left my cushy corporate job, teaming up with a friend who was at the centre of the ".com" boom, a boom which had subsequently gone bust.

We created a software business founded on my learning from my PepsiCo days: a business that would help managers understand their customers like never before and build an exciting customer-centric context for performance. Our goal was to disrupt mystery shopping and provide 50 times the data for the same price. At the time, mystery shopping was seen by many brands as being unrepresentative of the customer experience and unfair by many managers; and thus it often detracted from the context.

The concept caught on like wildfire. Our process was simple: invite customers on receipt of their bill to complete a survey on their experience, incentivising them with a small reward for doing so. Thereafter, we would supply all the reporting required at every level of the organisation over the Internet, to be accessed by using nothing other than a browser – we were software-as-a-service before the name was invented. The best part for our customers was that we provided 25-to-50 times the data from real customers for the same price as mystery shopping. A number that was statistically predictive of all the transactions in a location over the month, a number that was generated by real customers and a number that local managers would agree was fair.

It was quite a journey indeed. Our solution became more robust as the years progressed. We added advanced loyalty modelling, sales growth modelling, a number of new software features and a patented social-media promotion engine. In ten years we grew to 180 employees in Canada, the US and the UK and had the privilege of serving some of the world's most trusted retail and foodservice brands including: Citibank, McDonald's, Boots, Tesco, Exxon, Starbucks, Pizza Hut, ASDA and Brinker, to name a few. Our software was being used in more than 50 countries and 25 languages… people all around the globe were talking about their 'Empathica scores'. One such brand was our first customer in the UK, a customer who will always hold a special place in my memory: it was Mitchells and Butlers, and Tony Hughes and Adam Martin were the executive sponsors of our programme.

Mitchells and Butlers were among an elite group of sophisticated customers who worked with our analytics team to really uncover the causal link between customer satisfaction and sales improvements. A rough estimate for most brands was that a five per cent lift in customer satisfaction would result in a two per cent lift in sales. Even more interesting was the variance in performance among the best and worst locations within a brand, where it was not unusual to find the top-performing quartile of locations in satisfaction grow sales five-to-ten times faster than the bottom-performing quartile.

In working with these leading brands, I was brought back to the place where my journey began. Having created a fair and highly predictive metric of operational execution and customer satisfaction, we now had the context to determine how some local managers were able to outperform the rest. After years of observing best-practice managers, talking with brands and modelling performance across a number of dimensions at the local level, I came to confirm my original hypothesis – great managers get great results. *Great managers model many, if not all of the competencies outlined in this book!*

In Chris and Tony's previously published book, *Effective Brand Leadership*, they rightly acknowledge that companies require different leadership at different stages of growth. In 2013, I decided that my time had come and we sold Empathica to a US competitor (merged and now called InMoment), which is growing the business on an epic global scale.

Although we sold the business, I continued to be obsessed with the challenge of helping local leaders create a compelling context for their teams and joined Nudge Rewards with the belief that software could help average managers become great leaders – leaders who master the competencies required by eMOTION.

Nudge Rewards uses mobile software to empower and enable brands to communicate effectively with their local teams. Our ultimate goal is to provide local leaders with the tools they need to become inspirational leaders, using software to help them create a compelling context for work: a context that enables their managers and teams to achieve exceptional performance. Our software provides team members with tweet-like nudges, performance challenges and rewards to their mobile devices.

We believe that we are onto something big at Nudge, because there is a new generation of employees in retail and foodservice. This generation of millennials has grown up with technology and interacts with the world in a very different manner than prior generations. They check their mobile devices more than 150 times per day, take and publish 1,000s of pictures a year, seldom talk on the phone and maintain social networks that are ten times the size of their parents'. Capturing their hearts and minds will require a different approach: it will require us to use media that they use in their everyday lives.

With all these changes in how millennials utilise technology, we don't believe that their needs at work are any different from those of their parents. They need connection, they need a challenge and they want to be recognised for doing a great job. Millennials, like all employees, need and want a compelling context for work, orchestrated by a competent likeable management team. At Nudge we are pushing the boundaries of social media, mobile technology and gamification to assist brands and managers to orchestrate a compelling context for work and high performance. Using software to support managers in delivering on the promise outlined in *Inspirational Leadership*.

I first met Tony in 2006 and our paths have converged yet again, drawn together on a lifelong journey to uncover the drivers of performance excellence and empower those who are entrusted to deliver it. I believe that *Inspirational Leadership* and eMOTION represent a sea change, placing emotional outcomes on an equal footing with prior leadership movements. A change that could have only been brought to the fore by seasoned industry veterans. This book makes the unconscious competencies of inspirational leaders clear to all, teaching us that leadership is about more than things and numbers: it's about people, it's about leading through inspiration, capturing their hearts and imagination in every stage of their employment lifecycle, and mobilising them and their team by coaching courageously.

Since my first meeting with Tony (in a brilliant gastro pub of his creation), I knew he had a unique and special insight into the human side of management. Reflecting on Tony and Chris's careers leaves no doubt that they will be recognised as two of the industry's most influential executives of their time.

I hope you enjoy this fine piece of work as much as I have, and in conclusion I will leave you with one of my favourite quotes, from anthropologist Margaret Meade, who said:

> Never doubt that a small group of thoughtful, committed citizens can change the world: indeed, it's the only thing that ever has.

May your business be full of small groups of thoughtful, committed super-performing teams mobilised by inspirational leaders that practice eMOTION. Now, read on…

Contents

CONCLUSION – eMOTION and INSPIRATIONAL LEADERSHIP

List of Figures

About the Authors

Professor Chris Edger is the author of *Effective Multi-Unit Leadership - Local Leadership in Multi-Site Situations* (described by the *Leadership and Organization Development Journal* as "one of the key books of its kind for this decade"), *International Multi-Unit Leadership - Developing Local Leaders in International Multi-Site Operations, Professional Area Management - Leading at a Distance in Multi-Unit Enterprises* (two editions), *Franchising - How Both Sides Can Win* (shortlisted for the 2016 CMI Management Book of the Year and rated a 'Top 5 Must Read' book on franchising by Reed Commercial in June 2016), *Effective Brand Leadership - Be Different. Stay Different. Or Perish* (with Tony Hughes) and *Retail Area Management - Strategic and Local Models for Driving Growth*. Described by some commentators as the UK's leading expert on multi-site retail management, Chris frequently features in the media having appeared on and/or written for outlets such as Channel 4 News, ITV, BBC News Online, City A.M., Propel Info, *Retail Gazette, Daily Mail, Guardian, Telegraph, Retail Week, Which?* and *Drapers*. Previously, Chris had a successful career in the retail and service industry spanning 23 years, incorporating many senior positions in UK and internationally owned organisations. At the turn of the century, he was a member of an executive board that transacted two major cross-border FMCG drinks deals worth £2.3bn and $1.7bn, respectively. He holds a PhD (ESRC Award) from the Warwick Business School, an MSc (ECON) with distinction from the London School of Economics, an MBA and PGDip from NBS, and a Level 7 Advanced Award in Coaching and Mentoring (with distinction) and is a Fellow of the CIPD. Having founded the Academy of Multi-Unit Leadership in 2009, he has taught and coached leaders at post-graduate level at a number of Universities including the Warwick Business School (winning several MBA teaching excellence awards), the University of Birmingham and Birmingham City University.

Tony Hughes started in the hospitality industry with Stranneylands in 1967. Following a spell as Operations Manager for Duttons Restaurants in the north west of England, he moved south as Operations Director of Beefeater Steakhouses. Over a 22-year career with Whitbread Plc, he had numerous responsibilities, not least acquiring and establishing TGI Friday's in the UK. After a spell as Director of Quality at B&Q, Tony joined Bass Plc in December 1995 (now Mitchells and Butlers Plc), becoming the board director responsible for developing brands such as Toby, Vintage Inns, Premium County Dinning, Village Pub & Kitchen, Miller & Carter and acquiring Harvester, Browns and Alex in Germany. He is widely credited with transforming Mitchells and Butlers into the country's leading pub and restaurant branded company during his time in post. A luminary of the UK food service sector, he was awarded the Hotel & Caterer 'Catey', voted the Retailers' Retailer 'Best Individual' by the pub and restaurant industry in both 2002 and 2006 and received a Lifetime Achievement Award from the European Foodservice Summit in Zurich in 2007. After retiring from Mitchells and Butlers in 2008, Tony held non-executive positions in Russian and UK food service organisations. Having jointly authored *Effective Brand Leadership - Be Different. Stay Different. Or Perish* with Chris, Tony now devotes his time and energy to both writing and mentoring talent within the UK retail, hospitality and service industries.

Acknowledgements and Thanks

The authors would like to thank all the contributors to this book: in particular Nick Wylde, Managing Partner, Stanton Chase, who provided us with access to his Gamechanging Leadership series and Associate Professor Stephen Willson for insights from his Organic Growth podcast series. Both authors would like to thank Paul Charity, MD and Editor of Propel Info, and Paul Jervis, Managing Editor of Libri Publishing, for their great support during the process of researching and writing this book.

CHRIS WOULD LIKE TO DEDICATE THIS BOOK TO THE HUNDREDS OF MANAGERS AND EXECUTIVES HE HAS TAUGHT AND COACHED ON HIS MULTI-UNIT LEADERSHIP AND STRATEGY PROGRAMME OVER THE LAST DECADE. I HAVE LEARNT MUCH FROM YOU ALL. THANKS FOR INSPIRING ME!

TONY WOULD LIKE TO DEDICATE THIS BOOK TO HIS WIFE, GLYNIS, FOR BRINGING LIGHT, LOVE AND LAUGHTER TO HIS LIFE AND TO HIS CHILDREN, RICHARD AND KATHRYN, FOR GIVING HIM PURPOSE.

'Great leaders move us. They ignite our passion and inspire the best in us. When we try to explain why they are so effective, we speak of strategy, vision or powerful ideas. But the reality is much more primal. Great leadership works through the emotions...'

Daniel Goleman

TGI FRIDAY'S AND HOSEA THE GUACAMOLE MAN – INSPIRATIONAL LEADERSHIP THAT MOVED ME

Tony Hughes

Did Friday's change my life as a leader? *Absolutely*. And I can pinpoint the moment for you - pinpoint the exact moment! I was doing the DLC (Daily Labour Control) in a store office as part of my training and the Regional Manager, Fred Hultz, came in and said:

> "What are you doing?"
> "The DLC," I replied and Fred said:
> "Come on, let's catch somebody doing something right!"
> "Oh, interesting!" I thought.

So we went through the kitchen and walked past a nice Mexican chap who's making guacamole with the menu out, the recipe book out and all the correct ingredients, well turned out in a pristine uniform. So Fred calls an all-store meeting. All the staff gather together and Fred starts to explain:

> "I'd like to take this opportunity… because I've seen something today that I regret and feel guilty about. We have an employee that works in our kitchen that has come in here for the last six years every day making the most fabulous guacamole. Even though he knows exactly how to do it he's always got his recipe book open, he's got everything measured, he's got quality ingredients which he's inspected and you know what – you have the pleasure to serve fabulous guacamole and the guests have the honour to eat it. This guy is a backbone of this organisation and we are guilty of taking him for granted – we need to say thank you!"

Of course, everyone knew who Fred was talking about. People were so *moved* that tears had started flooding down their faces and this poor chap was beside himself. Then Fred said:

"Hosea, we all want you to know how much we appreciate you and the quality of your work. Consistent high performance is often taken for granted and the spectacular one offs acclaimed by the crowd, but to the team, the true heroes are hidden heroes who go about their work in a consistent, dependable and predictable manner, unselfishly working for the benefit of others. These are truly our most valuable players..."

Fred then produced an MVP (Most Valuable Person) medal and pinned it on Hosea's chest in military fashion, shook his hand and hugged him to huge applause and cheering from all the restaurant staff.

It was very *emotional* and, you know, at that moment I realised that I'd spent the first part of my life in senior management thinking that my job was to stop people doing things wrong... but it's not! It's a leader's role to catch people doing things right and *inspire others to do likewise*. That's what changed my life.

BRIEF INTRODUCTION

We have written this book for anybody who leads people. Not just those that lead large companies: anyone who has people responsibilities, large or small. It is written for leaders who are determined to improve their leadership skills through leveraging *our concept of eMOTION*. That is, *inspiring people by shifting feelings from negative into positive states*; *moving* them to do good and find fulfilment, and *generating* a passion to work as a team to build something of meaning and significance. In short, *mobilising* super-performing teams and individuals!

Relax, this is not an academic treatise on leadership. What we seek to do with this book is inspire you to look at how you lead in a slightly different way. A lot of leadership text books talk about concepts such as transformational leadership, engagement, empowerment and commitment as means by which you can energise and mobilise teams. In order to operate in these enlightened ways, they suggest that leaders require high levels of emotional intelligence. We certainly don't disagree with many of these theories and approaches. But what we believe is that – fundamentally – leading people successfully is all about subtly *nudging and shifting feelings*. People who *feel* good about themselves and their work are more likely to care about their customers. Customers who *feel* that the people they are dealing with *care* are more likely to trust the organisation they are buying goods and services from. As a result they buy more and are more loyal. It stands to reason, therefore, that the primary role of a leader is to create the climate within which their people *feel* happy and motivated. This means that leaders must always pay attention to the ways and means by which they can *shift feelings to harness positive emotions*.

But how do inspirational leaders shift feelings to create super-performing teams and individuals? This book addresses this question in four parts:

- First, by highlighting the *four qualities* that inspirational leaders require to generate positive emotions amongst their people
- Second, by outlining and describing eMOTION, namely the ten moments of emotional truth that leaders need to attend to during the *cycle of employment* in order to shift feelings and move people in order to mobilise super-performance

- Third, by outlining a number of courageous coaching techniques that leaders can apply on a one-to-one basis to build *accountability*, raise *awareness* and *reframe perspectives* amongst their direct reports, so that they are happier, more productive and achieve their personal and organisational goals
- Finally, by outlining the *importance and significance of emotion* both generally and in organisational life.

We do not pretend that this book can lay claim to be the first or final word on leadership. What we want it to do – by laying out our philosophy gathered over years of 'doing' and researching the subject – is to make you stop and think. What am I fundamentally trying to achieve as a leader? What qualities do I need? How can I *move* and inspire my people *to feel good*, delighting our internal and external customers more effectively? How can I generate enduring super-performance that outstrips the competition? This book will hopefully provide some of the answers you seek to those questions.

Inspirational Leadership Qualities

Behavioural scientists believe that humans are physiologically and neurologically primed to react to seven dominant feelings: anger, sadness, fear, surprise, disgust, contempt and happiness. Additionally, they have observed that emotional reflexes are *far* quicker than our cognitive thinking patterns, moving us - due to primal survival and pleasure instincts - to react to our feelings more rapidly than to rational thought. It stands to reason, therefore, that leaders who are able to generate *positive feelings* (and neutralise negative feelings) amongst their people stand a far better chance of securing outstanding behaviours. Dry logic rarely (or slowly) stimulates; *sensory appeal rapidly galvanises*. The following chapters will outline how inspirational leaders drive eMOTION through activating positive feelings during ten fundamental 'moments of emotional truth' and courageous coaching; *but* what personal *qualities* do they require to lead in this way? We believe that, in addition to meeting generic technical, behavioural and cognitive requirements, these leaders have four distinct qualities that have *emotional resonance*: inspirational leaders are spiritual, holistic, optimistic and proactive. These four qualities are expanded upon in turn below.

SPIRITUAL

The first quality that great leaders have is a high degree of spirituality that inspires those around them. What do we mean by this? We are not inferring that inspirational leaders are raving 'Moonie', cult figures, narcissistically brainwashing followers with nefarious motives of power and exploitation. What we believe is that great leaders harness the emotions of their people by appealing to their souls, giving them a sense of real meaning and direction underpinned by a strong sense of morality. To this extent they exhibit two main characteristics, namely: a heartfelt purpose and cast-iron values.

- **Heartfelt purpose** - inspirational leaders have a clear heartfelt purpose which inspires *deep feelings of hope*, creating deep bonds of attachment and loyalty. In short, they stand for and articulate something powerful and worthwhile. They have a sense of destiny and believe themselves to be custodians of a noble cause which attracts buy-in and loyal followership. This quality is an absolutely fundamental prerequisite of inspirational leaders, because of the unending human search for meaning. Man has worshipped gods and icons since the dawn of time in an attempt to give their lives some sense of higher meaning. Humans constantly ask themselves: what is it all for, what is the *purpose* of my existence? The workplace – given the amount of time people spend there – plays a large part in human identity and can go some way in providing answers to these questions. Inspirational leaders recognise this by tapping into these existential emotions by making their teams feel that they are special. They make their teams feel elite – different and better than the rest, part of an important journey, builders of an exciting future.

- **Cast-iron values** – this heartfelt purpose is underpinned by cast-iron values: sincerely expressed and grounded in integrity. The inspirational leader has a strong moral code which (s)he models through their behaviours and decision-making patterns. They are constant and consistent in what they say and do, which generates *intense feelings of trust* and respect amongst their followers. It also enables them to impose a degree of ideological rather than bureaucratic control in the organisation, because people have become instinctively programmed to know 'how to do the right thing' rather than 'just doing it right'. In short, the inspirational leader – through their moral behaviour and demeanour – creates intentional and purposeful behaviours within their teams and/or organisation that will result in assured outcomes. Great leaders know that their followers cannot take a manual out onto the floor when they deal with customers and despatch their tasks – rather they need to be imbued with a strong sense of right and wrong in order to make the right choices for themselves, their customers and –ultimately – the organisation.

CASE STUDY 1 – **MAKING SAINSBURY'S GREAT AGAIN**
JUSTIN KING, FORMER CEO, SAINSBURY'S

Justin King was CEO of Sainsbury's, one of the UK's top three grocery chains, for ten years. When he took over in 2004, there were doubts that the chain would survive given its catastrophic collapse in profit and market share under previous management. Implementing his turnaround plan, 'Making Sainsbury's Great Again', King increased sales during his tenure from £16.5bn to £26.3bn, profit from £249m to £798m and customer transactions from 14m to 24m per week. In 2014 he was voted 'Most Admired Leader' by his peers in the Management Today Most Admired Companies Award. Previously Justin had occupied senior positions at M&S Food, Häagen Dazs, Asda, PepsiCo and Mars.

Sainsbury's as a business had truly once been a great business. If one goes back to the mid-1980s it would have been seen – by common consent – as one of, if not *the* leading grocery businesses in the world. John Sainsbury, the CEO and Chairman at the time would have been regarded as the leading light of his generation. He was an *inspirational leader* who really got the customer; in fact, he had a knack of getting the customer before the customer got themselves!

But it became a business that lost its way because it had *stopped putting customers at the heart of everything it did*. Why? In the 1990s a new management regime concluded that Sainsbury's had the best sites, that 30k sq ft was the optimal supermarket footprint and that the UK grocery market was becoming saturated. So they looked at diversifying abroad and into non-food. But their analysis was wrong. While Sainsbury's were 'aiming off', Tesco reinvented the supermarket over a period of ten years, surpassing Sainsbury's as the number one grocer in the UK in 1995.

So when I arrived at Sainsbury's in 2004 the business had lost market share for about 14 years in a row because, I would argue: first, it had lost consumer focus (at least partly through the loss of its inspirational leader, John Sainsbury); second, it had diverted resources away from the core of the business so it was satisfying customers less well over time; and third, in an attempt to address that failure over time, it set about a journey around 1999–2000 in a way that customers *couldn't* accept.

There wasn't a lot wrong with the turnaround plan that the business originally started in 2000 in terms of its identification of the issues faced by the business but they made the mistake of promising that the change would happen with no expense to shareholders. Now that kind of change – if it's at *no* expense to shareholders – must be at the expense of customers. So prices were less sharp, availability was poor... availability was poor because the systems changes were being done in a rapid way which meant that the service levels couldn't be maintained and the business was overly tight on cost because the top line had stopped growing as a result of all those changes. The way I like to describe it is that what we had basically done is *ask our customers to indulge us through this very difficult period* of change. And our customers said to us: "we might come back when you've sorted it out, but in the meantime there's lots of other places we can do our shopping, thanks very much!"

So the idea of 'Making Sainsbury's Great Again' really came from listening to how our customers and colleagues in the business were *feeling* at that time. Customers *felt* that "this was once a great place to shop where I *loved* doing my weekly grocery shop and I'd really *love* to come back and do that again". And our colleagues felt that they "used to be proud to work here. I *loved* working here. I'd tell my friends that I was here and I would envisage the rest of my career here. But now I hope nobody asks me where I work because I don't want to admit it". So 'Making Sainsbury's Great Again' was all about "we're going to take the business back to that *feeling* for you – our customers and colleagues!" So how did we do it?

- **Senior leadership change** – the top leader group in our business – 1,000 or so leaders (including the store managers) – stayed largely as I had found it. Four years into our turnaround, 95 per cent of the people were still there. There was a very simple reason for that. I had found a lot of really good people who knew how to do their jobs really well but there had been a real failure of senior leadership: and so most of the 40 or so senior people changed. That was pretty much all of the Plc board and operating board. But beyond that, there was no more than natural turnover in the ranks below. Some people went naturally on to do other things and we recruited some great people in their stead. And by providing that *clarity of direction*, some good personal leadership as well (I'd like to claim my part, if you like, in this success!) we re-energised what was actually a fantastic team that had been badly led.

- **Shareholder buy-in** – in October 2004 we articulated to shareholders how we thought we could grow sales and how long it would take profits to recover because of the money we needed to invest in the customer service offer – in pricing and in quality. By laying it out over time with key stage posts, shareholders could check in along the way, monitoring that we were achieving what we'd said we'd do. I found the shareholders to be very supportive. I think that management has to be very clear that in the end they manage the business and I would say that one of the first steps on the slippery road to disaster is management starting to do things because they believe that shareholders want them to do it rather than management believing that it's the right thing to do. As you'll gather from my view of the world, *as long as you're focused on customers and colleagues*, then that's almost inevitably going to reap rewards for the corporation and therefore serve the best interests of the shareholders!

- **Legendary behaviour** – the only place you service customers in grocery (including online and digital) is in your shops. How did I instil this passion back into the business? I became reasonably *famous* for my first day at Sainsbury's. I didn't turn up at what Sainsbury's called 'Head Office', I turned up at a shop – the number one store in the company. At about 9 a.m. I got a call on my mobile from the HR Director saying "Er, Justin it's the 28th March and you appear not to have turned up for work!" I said "I have, I'm in a shop and – by the way – I've been here a couple of hours and been expecting your phone call." Now clearly I was – symbolically – trying to send a message. It was a point that needed to be made. *The only place we serve customers is in our shops.* The only people serving customers were our colleagues within those shops. And – in truth – the organisation was doing a lamentable job of equipping colleagues to serve customers: we needed to change the centre of gravity of the business. I understood this and empowering the operating side of the business was a key part of the change we made. The message was in my actions on that first day. Many of the store managers subsequently said to me that that behaviour alone (visiting a store on the first minute of my first day) made them *feel* stronger than they'd *felt* for a long time in the organisation.

- **Potent symbolism** – we also set about changing the names of our offices. They were all called 'Head Office' or a 'Regional Office': they were all changed to be called 'Store Support Centres' – places where we support the stores. But we didn't just change the plaque over the door, we said "when you achieve these things and are rated for providing support to the stores than you have earned the right to be called a Store Support Centre". So, for example, we set targets about how quickly and frequently phones were answered when a store called, how soon an answer to the store question was provided… and so our depots, regional offices and Head Office in Holborn all earned the right to be called a Store Support Centre…

- **Communicating and listening** – I set up mechanisms whereby I met with every store manager every quarter for my entire ten years, at 20 or 30 at a time, plus getting the 600 of them together once a year as part of the National Conference. So I met with 20-to-30 of them face to face, with none of their regional management present – just them – telling them a bit about what I was thinking, giving them a chance to ask me questions, but also as an opportunity to tell me what was going on. Famously, in one of the very first meetings (and this is in a book by Gurnek Bains who was with me at the time because we were using him as a consultant on culture) I got to the last of 15-or-so meetings I'd had across the country and I remember saying to Gurnek, "I'm not getting this, because I'm just not hearing the *anger*, bile and frustration that I should be on behalf of the colleagues and customers – and these are who are store managers represent." I was quite worried. If our store managers aren't shouting, how am I going to get this business 'up for it'? And to this day I'm absolutely convinced it was deliberate but… as the last group left, placed on the front row was a piece of paper and I walked over and picked it up: and it was an email from one of the regional managers (who wasn't in the room, of course) and it said "following our conference call today – here are the questions we've agreed to ask Justin"! It was then I realised that even the people responsible for the regional operations of the business had become part of the problem.

- **Empowering colleagues** – so we had to empower the store managers, which I did through regular contact, and *also* empower our colleagues in the stores through a suggestion scheme called 'Tell Justin'. During my tenure we had about 70,000 or so suggestions from colleagues! For the first six months, I answered every one personally. For the rest of my time there these were answered by a director but I promised that *I* would answer every customer and colleague letter that came *directly* addressed to me. My team told me – as I left – that I'd answered 2.9 letters a day for every day in the previous ten years. There were some great ideas and you always find out stuff that had not been brought to the attention of the board.

- **Taming bureaucracy** – the final point I'd make is that, structurally, Operations had equal representation around the Operational Board (with Finance, HR, Marketing etc.). Obviously all the divisions had their part to fulfil and the job of directors was to ensure that games were not played further down the organisation. Because by its very nature, bureaucracy will tend to do the types of things one would imagine. Humans are that way inclined and one needs to be mindful of it. For instance, in the early days we had logistics and retail as two separate divisions. But I couldn't get to the bottom of why they appeared to be separate divisions at all, when I thought they should be lining up together to serve customers. So I decided that what we would have to do is put them into the same director and it solved the problem overnight. Because once both divisions knew that they were marching to the beat of the same director, it's amazing the difference that it made. Sometimes, if there are unnecessary arguments, you make sure the structure of the organisation is right because there's this natural tendency to defend your piece of piece of turf even if the whole is more important than the sum of its parts...

HOLISTIC

The second quality of inspirational leaders is their ability to provide coherence through taking a balanced, holistic approach. They can see how all the moving parts of their organisation *fit* together to harmoniously form the greater whole. This is particularly important in service-based contexts where breakdowns in one area of the operation can have unintended effects elsewhere. Also, they are quick to neutralise negative emotions such as fear, anxiety and anger amongst their teams through their ability to spot and fix deadly combinations. Above all, they appreciate the contributions of all their team – assimilating and melding rather than fracturing through 'divide and rule'. These holistic attributes manifest themselves in two main characteristics:

- **Tacit knowledge** – inspirational leaders have a holistic quality that is underpinned by deep tacit knowledge that engenders a *feeling of confidence* amongst their team. What is this tacit knowledge and why is it important? Tacit knowledge (unlike explicit knowledge) is generally uncodified and unarticulated within organisations. It is 'how things really work around here'. Inspirational leaders gain a deep understanding of how all the moving parts fit together either through prior learning or intense immersion. Why is this important? Several studies have shown that the most successful leaders have a flexible learning mindset rather than a fixed one. This ability to drill down and figure out how things tie in with one another gives them the ability to abandon any prejudices or preconceived ideas that they might have had that could have held them and the organisation back. It is important because of the constantly evolving nature of business and competitive threat. Leaders who do not possess a real tacit knowledge and understanding of their operation's 'ecosystem' will make decisions that will result in significant missteps that could take months or years to put right. But having this tacit knowledge, being able to ask team members the right questions, identifying where things can be improved and understanding the unintended consequences of certain actions not only strengthens the business: it creates real feelings of trust and confidence amongst their team. It reinforces a feeling amongst followers that they are being led by somebody who is a competent professional rather than a clueless opportunist.

- **Inclusive mentality** – but inspirational leaders recognise that they cannot do it all themselves and that the 'whole is greater than its sum of parts'. What do we mean by this? Leaders inspire their teams to *feel wanted and valued* by involving subordinates in decision making (at the appropriate time) and also through propagating a 'one team' mentality. To this extent, they set up their organisation to succeed by respecting the contributions of *all* team-members, in whatever function or department. They clamp down on splinter groups and cliques. In short, what they create through this inclusive mentality is a *strong feeling of tribal identity and cohesion*. So, in addition to the psychological buy-in they have fostered through a sense of spirituality (see above), they also create a powerful feeling of social community where an 'all for one and one for all' attitude prevails.

CASE STUDY 2 – **GAMECHANGING LEADERSHIP**
PETER LONG, CHAIRMAN, TUI

Peter Long is the Chairman of TUI, Europe's largest tourism business (with sales of £16bn per annum). In 1996, having become the Managing Director of First Choice, he led the turnaround of the company, subsequently overseeing its merger with TUI and becoming CEO of the combined enterprise. The merger was a great success and Peter is acknowledged to have masterfully stewarded the company through the 2007–12 global economic crisis and digital disruption that has radically changed consumer behaviour within this sector.

In 1996 when I joined First Choice, I found that this was a company that had a significant market position and had been rebranded *but was badly run*. I believed I could fix it and that we could improve the business: that was the attraction for me. How did we do it?

- **Clarity** – you have to have a clear plan of how you are going to get there – and for me it was quite simple. First, ensure that we sold the appropriate number of holidays profitably (in our industry, too much capacity gives you huge problems). Second, ensure that we bought our hotel capacity in the most efficient way with the right numbers and at the right price. Third, ensure we had a cost structure that was appropriate for the size of the business. And when you put all those elements together, you bolster the operational integrity of the business! That was the plan and that is what we executed immediately. This level of clarity was essential to enable execution.

- **Knowledgeable team** – every business needs *a strong team*. It's not about individuals – it's about *teamwork*. You normally find in any business that there are some great operational people: and that's what I found. The problem was at the senior-leader level, in terms of the direction they had previously set the business. So we had to identify and use the *talents of strong internal people* who were supplemented by some external expertise. Probably the best recruit at that time was Richard Prosser. He made a huge difference because he under*stood 'overseas'* and the whole overseas operation. He and I talked the same language straight away.

- **Strategy** – the industry needed to consolidate, so how could we participate in that consolidation? Our view was very clear: we could either sell our mainstream First Choice business and keep the specialist portfolio or merge with another player. What happened in terms of the sequence of events was that two potential buyers, Thomas Cook and Airtours, decided to merge; so neither was any longer a potential buyer for us! But what happens when an industry consolidates is that one move often creates another move; and the other move in the case was that TUI and First Choice merged to create Europe's leading tourism business. (This would not have happened without the initial consolidation of Thomas Cook and Airtours.) And that was absolutely the right move for us. So we played a major part in the consolidation and we twin tracked one another through the Competition Commission process: they were about four weeks in front of us – and that's not for the fainthearted in terms of how the regulator might act! But because the industry had changed so much, particularly with the growth of online carriers, they said "this is not going to be in any way against the consumer because there are so many alternatives."

- **Simplicity** – TUI is big but it is not complex. Maybe I only say this because I've had 30 years in the industry. But it's broken down into very clear business units, with some very big leaders, divisional CEOs, leading entities that could be PLCs in their own right. But we run with a very flat structure and a very important, strong divisional set-up that makes the business very manageable. Our aim is to avoid complexity because, if you say to someone "it's all very difficult, it's a complex business", people will ask "why?" So our business is all about scale – power brands – but it's not about complexity.

OPTIMISTIC

The third major quality of inspirational leaders is infectious optimism, which is imitated by those around them. The link between positive thinking and optimal emotional states has long been established, as has the insight that humans – due to primal survival instincts – have a tendency towards negativity and scepticism. However, positivity creates positivity. It unleashes creativity and helps people transition through difficult times and events. Inspirational leaders recognise this. They are relentlessly optimistic about the present and future potential of both their teams and their organisation; they are 'glass half full' types (not delusionally but realistically so). Their enthusiasm and positivity is contagious at all levels of the organisation, enabling them to manage the short-term journey whilst guiding the organisation to its long-term destination. In essence, then, this vital quality of optimism is underpinned by two outstanding characteristics:

- **Positive mood** – Daniel Goleman pointed out in his seminal work on emotional intelligence that 'primal leaders' consistently maintained an 'optimistic, high energy mood'? What is this and why do we think it matters? In essence, inspiring leaders consciously or unconsciously recognise that positivity unburdens people from the downbeat constraints of negativity. People are more inclined to think and act with more clarity, energy and creativity if they are in a positive state of mind. If they feel good about what they are doing they are more inclined to care about the effect and impact of what they do. But this can only *consistently* manifest itself if the leader is him-/herself in a positive frame of mind. Why? Because followers are inclined to read the signals given off by their leader and imitate them. In short, employee moods are heavily influenced by their leader's emotional disposition. We recall a student who once said to one of us that working for a particular individual was tiring and debilitating as "he expected us to get excited on his behalf!" Working for people who are inclined towards pessimism, believing their followers should draw upon their own resources to act positively, is mentally draining. To bastardise a biblical phrase: blessed are the leaders that conduct themselves with a cheery smile and positive outlook on circumstances, for they shall inherit unswerving loyalty.

- **Growth mindset** – in her thought-provoking book, *Mindset: How You Can Fill Your Potential*, the eminent psychologist Carole Dweck discriminated between people who had a *fixed* and those who had a *growth* mindset. The former tended to exhibit high levels of negativism, conservatism and resistance to change whilst the latter group displayed positivity, flexibility and high levels of curiosity. Growth mindset individuals, she observed, outperformed those with a fixed one. We agree with her insights, arguing that almost all the inspirational leaders we have known and observed display this trait. Leaders with a growth mindset brim with optimism, scanning the horizon for possibilities, accepting – on occasion – that the battle might be lost, but the war is still there to be won. They do not dwell on mistakes; rather, they learn from them and incorporate these learnings into their future projects and campaigns. The effect that such a mindset has on followers is profound, instilling *feelings of restless curiosity and unfettered ambition.*

CASE STUDY 3 – **INSPIRATIONAL LEADERSHIP QUALITIES**
NICK WYLDE, MANAGING PARTNER, STANTON CHASE

Nick Wylde has recruited and placed outstanding talent within the C-suites of Europe's largest consumer-facing brands for over a quarter of a century. An alumnus of Cornell University, Nick is also a widely respected commentator on game-changing leadership.

I am going to do three things. First, highlight what I believe inspirational leaders do well. Second, bring these factors to life by reflecting upon the qualities of someone I regard as an exemplary modern-day leader, namely Angela Ahrendts, ex-CEO of Burberry and now at Apple. Third, consider how leadership requirements have changed over the last 30 years.

- **What are inspirational leaders?** – through close interaction, observation and empirical analysis of the best (and worst!) I believe great leaders are:
  - *Fantastic communicators* – they are influential throughout the organisation: they frame the tone and agenda *positively and optimistically*

- *Confident change generators* – they are innovators, confidently addressing changes in market and customer needs to *drive growth*
- *Great team builders and delegators* – they build great teams which they empower to deliver against mutually agreed parameters
- *Agents of simplicity rather than complexity* – they have this uncanny knack of clarity and getting to the heart of things; breaking things down into bite-sized, understandable chunks
- *Calm, poised and resilient* – they are able to take the right decisions under enormous pressure
- *Challengers of the status quo* – they constantly challenge orthodox ways of doing things in a quest to do things 'better, faster, smarter'
- *Humble, receptive and reasoned* – they are great listeners, processing information rationally, with egoism rarely interfering.

- **The exemplary leader: Angela Ahrendts** – if push came to shove, I would single out Angela as one of the most outstanding inspirational leaders I have come across over the past 30 years. Why? She transformed a small British luxury brand that, prior to her arrival in 2006, had been principally known for its trench coats, umbrellas and Burberry check, into a global powerhouse by the time of her departure in 2014. Through her clear vision and ability to surround herself with talented people, she powered Burberry to the top table of international luxury brands. If I had to pick three qualities she had which stood out? First, her outstanding *communication skills*. Every week she spoke directly to her people using the latest digital technology, telling them what the business was trying to do and giving them a heartfelt thanks for their crucial role in Burberry's success. She really *loved* her employees. Second, she had a *strong will to win and succeed*, both in terms of *growing* the business and *growing* employees. She really was a cheerleader for momentum, growth and success. Third, she was *committed to innovation*, driving Burberry into the digital age and turning it into a multi-channel company, stealing a march on her competitive set.

- **Leaders 'then and now'** – when I look back 30 years, the characteristics that blighted many 'captains of industry' at that time – arrogance, egoism, bullying – are no longer workable in today's environment. In this digital, fast-paced era, accountability and transparency are the order of the day. The business terrain is too dynamic in consumer-facing business for corporations to be run by unaccountable potentates. Inspirational leaders have a strong innovation and *growth agenda*, surround themselves with great people and instil a *positive*, agile culture within their organisations. To end, let me tell you a story. Some years ago I was approached to find a leader for a large consumer-facing business. The business was failing. The previous leader was renowned for being chauffeured into work, opening the car door, entering the building and then taking the lift up to his office. At the end of the day he did the same thing in reverse. The new leader I had a hand in appointing did the opposite. He revelled in touring the office, talking to people – picking up on their hopes, feelings, fears, desires and aspirations. He listened and also explained. Today, led by the same person, that business is the outstanding company in its respective sector. So to summarise, in my view: inspirational leadership is close rather than distant, responsible rather than detached, tough at times – yes – but always for the right reasons *and* in the best interests of customers and employees.

PROACTIVE

Finally, in tandem with the qualities above, inspirational leaders ooze urgency, energy and pace. They proactively observe, challenge, rectify and follow up. In short, they are 'on the case', without squeezing autonomous behaviour out of the organisation. They are 'in' the business rather than 'on' it. This enables them to run at problems, rather than run away from them, encouraging the same behaviours from their teams. Again, this behaviour minimises any feelings of immobilisation, inertia and fear that might paralyse the organisation when things are perceived to be going wrong. They have the ability to turn negative sentiments into positive feelings (such as gratitude and enthusiasm) because they are actively willing to do something to sort things out quickly. Again, we would identify two main characteristics that underpin this quality:

- **Black box thinking** – in his fantastic book, *Black Box Thinking*, the writer and media commentator Mathew Syed outlined how the aviation industry had dramatically improved safety by encouraging a culture of problem disclosure. Pilots are encouraged to report malfunctions and incidents without threat of sanction, so that the industry can learn and lock-in improvements. He contrasted this with another sector, the healthcare industry. Here, particularly in hospitals, professional elites (i.e. surgeons and consultants) conspired to keep missteps secret for reasons of 'Hippocratic arrogance' and/or fear of the threat of legal sanctions. Syed contrasted those hospitals with high levels of error disclosure during the course of daily operations with those that had a low level. Interestingly, the former had a lower level of patient mortality than the latter. Reporting mistakes, understanding their origins, rectifying their root causes and systemising them had a profound effect on quality and resilience. But such approaches, clearly, had to become rooted in culture. We believe that the best leaders are those who encourage black box thinking, where people can raise issues and concerns that relate to operations in the knowledge that they will not be sanctioned or admonished for doing so. Equally importantly, inspirational leaders will proactively follow up and chase down problems to set the dynamic tone for the organisation. Such actions generally propagating *feelings of relief and gratitude* amongst team members that – at last – 'something is being done to sort things out'.

- **Simplicity focus** – their proactive nature not only compels them to confront and to solve, but also to embed simplicity. What do we mean by this? Organisations become complex entities as they grow larger. A larger structure brings with it greater hierarchy, more bureaucracy and (almost inevitably) slower, more ponderous decision making. Inspirational leaders know how to 'cut the crap', reduce non-value-added behaviours and get people to focus on the one thing that keeps them in business, namely: *its customers' needs*. Leaders who re-engineer their organisations around the needs of their customers rather than factional, internal interests are more likely to be successful. By asking one simple question – does this activity add value to the customer experience? – they will achieve some degree of primacy over their competitive set. In doing so, they engender *feelings of delight and satisfaction* amongst their followers that, for once, 'somebody has got their priorities right'.

CASE STUDY 4 – **INSPIRING A MULTI-BRAND PORTFOLIO**
SIMON VINCENT, PRESIDENT, EMEA HILTON HOTELS

Over the past ten years, Simon has led the growth of Hilton across the EMEA region, spearheading the distribution of its multi-brand proposition (Conrad Resorts and Hotels, Waldorf Astoria Hotels, Doubletree by Hilton, Hilton Garden Inn, Hampton by Hilton and Curio and Canopy) across 54 countries. Simon was previously CEO of Opodo and Chief Operating Officer of Thomas Cook Travel.

If I look back to 2006 when I first agreed to join Hilton, it was a very different company. It was about to be acquired by Blackstone and over the course of the subsequent ten years, the company was transformed out of all recognition, particularly in my region. A large part of the transformation was taking our brands on to the international stage – a lot of our brands had hitherto been resident in the USA and a big part of our plan was to expand our global footprint. The business in Europe, Middle East and Africa played a big role in that.

After Blackstone's acquisition, transforming Hilton was a start-up situation in the sense that we really needed to reboot the business. In reality we were taking two businesses that has hitherto been distinct – we had Hilton International owned by Ladbrokes, listed on the London Stock Exchange, and Hilton Hotels Corporation which was owned by the Hilton family but also listed on the New York Stock Exchange. Blackstone brought the two businesses together and that's when the transformation started. You had two businesses that were at different stages of their evolution, both with very different business models. We needed to create a single identity for the business, align the organisation and its culture to really transform the business. I think we've succeeded in doing that over the course of the last ten years. So how was this success achieved?

- **Brands that are *loved*** – it is first and foremost about our brands. Customers love our brands. You only have to look at the customer feedback that we get and the REVPAR premiums that our brands enjoy over and above the competition. Each one of our individual brands enjoys a REVPAR premium over the completion in their respective customer segment.

- **Commercial engine** – our success has also been attributable to the strength of our commercial engine: our distribution systems, our sales, marketing and distribution capabilities.

- **People strength** – above everything, the strength of our people has driven our success. Hilton is known as a people organisation. We take great pride in training our people, putting them into leadership positions that allow them to grow and fulfil their potential in what is a great organisation. So – I think a combination of strong brands, a strong commercial engine and strong people really makes Hilton what it is today.

- **Simplicity and clarity** – underpinning all of this, we have a very clear vision to *spread the light and warmth of hospitality* and we have very clear strategic objectives. I think it is important that this strategy is very *simple* and *focused*. Our strategy was all around aligning our organisation around a single vision and culture. It was about maximising our performance: expanding our global footprint, taking our brands into the international arena. It was also about strengthening our brands and our commercial services platform. I think that aligning the whole organisation behind that single vision and those four strategic imperatives was a very powerful force in making it happen.

- **Hospitality and proactivity** – we are all about hospitality. 'We are hospitality. We are Hilton!' And that's what we aim to do. We aim to serve our guests and hopefully they'll come back and stay with us over a lifetime. I think our culture is absolutely defined by the word 'hospitality' but I think we also operate to very high levels of integrity. *We have a real sense of urgency in our business now, in terms of getting things done.* One of our values is *'Now!'*: living in the moment, making things happen, driving performance.

- **Distributing leadership** – our culture has definitely transformed over the course of the last few years, giving people accountability, encouraging people to lead their teams and lead them effectively, and really setting ambitious targets then letting people get on and deliver them. A big part of the philosophy is around distributing leadership – actually devolving decision making down to those parts of the organisation best placed to make those decisions. We are a global organisation now. We operate in more than 100 countries, we've got over 4,300 hotels – a lot of decision making has to be devolved down to the hotels and distributing leadership is a big part of facilitating that in our culture!

'I've learnt that people will forget what you said, people will forget what you did, but people will never forget how you made them feel…'

Maya Angelou

eMOTION #1
The Ten Moments of Emotional Truth

So the qualities that inspirational leaders require to shift feelings, change sentiments, transform attitudes and reframe perspectives from neutral or negative to positive states include various dimensions of *spirituality*, *holism*, *optimism* and *proactivity*. But what do inspirational leaders actually *do* to create eMOTION – mobilising positivity: *moving and shifting feelings* within their teams and organisations? The first thing to say is that a lot has been written about emotion within leadership and at the workplace. What broadly does this say?

Emotional labour – defined as jobs requiring emotional connection with others (retail, restaurants, service centres etc.); as emotional labour is valued less highly than highly skilled cognitive labour, exploitation often occurs (through unfair division of labour and alienation of workers), causing 'surface acting' amongst workers

Emotional climate – defines the culture of an organisation (with compliance or commitment-based spectrums)

Emotional intelligence – describes levels of leader self-awareness, self-control and awareness of others' needs/feelings

Emotional control – refers to levels of mental toughness and resilience: an ability to control negative and channel positive emotions

Emotional bank account – denotes the amount of currency/credit leaders have to exchange for worker discretionary effort

Emotional intensity – calibrates strength (low, medium, high) of positive or negative feelings that can affect intentions, behaviours and actions

Emotional buy-in – defines the degree to which hearts as well as minds are engaged within teams and organisations

Emotional distance – describes the degree of psychological attachment felt by employees according to geographical, structural and leader proximity

---

Figure 1 **Leadership and Workplace Emotion Definitions**

But our position is this: we acknowledge that much of the writing and research has greatly advanced our understanding of emotion in relation to both leader behaviour and workplace dynamics. However, we believe that we can broaden, and contribute to, the emotion debate. In our view there are *ten key leadership stages in the employment cycle* that can be isolated for emotional impact. These are *moments in the employment relationship where leaders actively seek to shift specific feelings for maximum effect, through specific actions*. Indeed, a failure to mobilise positive emotions at any one of these key stages of the cycle will lead to suboptimal outcomes. We call these stages in the cycle the Ten Moments of Emotional Truth for inspirational leaders, which are highlighted in our model below.

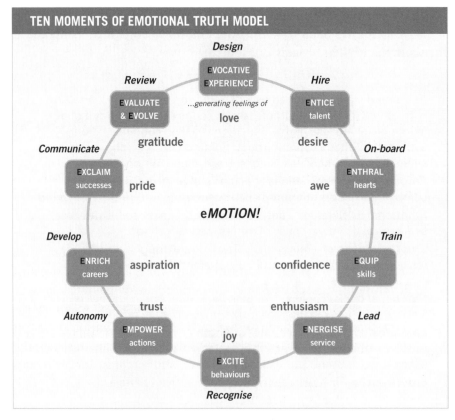

Figure 2 **The Ten Moments of Emotional Truth Model**

Why is every stage in the model so important and what do inspirational leaders do to shift positive feelings at these key moments of emotional truth? The next ten sections will address these two questions.

1. EVOCATIVE EXPERIENCE – Design (Generating LOVE)

The first key moment of truth for inspirational leaders is the design stage of the organisation. It is at this moment that the leader must fashion a product or service that amounts to a truly evocative experience for both the team and customers. All other moments of truth will fail unless this cornerstone is put in place. But what does 'evocative experience' mean? 'Evocative' implies positive imagery that sears itself into the *hearts and memories* of all participants and recipients. This is generated though positive experiences that stimulate and heighten all the major conscious and subconscious senses. Furthermore, what leaders achieve through designing an evocative experience is the transformation of ambient feelings of potential ***ambivalence*** towards their product or service into ***love***. This deep-seated attraction and attachment to what they have created results in high levels of retention, loyalty and advocacy of both staff and customers. Inspirational leaders understand the first maxim of successful brands and products: *design a quality product that your customers love and your team will love it too!*

But how do inspirational leaders turn feelings of (potential) ambivalence into love at this product/service design stage?

- **Stand for something good** – all successful products and services have one thing in common: they provide a *distinctive* solution to a customer problem. That is to say, they satisfy the unfulfilled needs, feelings and aspirations of hardworking people. They find a 'market place with a market space' either through luck or judgement. They are most successful when they aim for category leadership, developing focused, scalable offers that quickly gain 'first mover' pre-emptive status. In short, they find their game and they play it – they stand for something important. But the most important factor that sustains and nurtures success is the fact that, intrinsically, the product or brand stands for something of inherent goodness. It adds to the sum of human happiness.

- **Create a warm personality** – leaders must define the way in which their product brand will 'speak' and relate appealingly to its key stakeholder constituencies (customers, staff, partners, suppliers etc.). To this extent they aim to create a clear identity and warm theatrical personality with *soul* that resonates. This is commonly expressed through an evocative essence and the careful assembly of symbolic brand elements. In terms of *product essence*, (s)he can choose four or five words 'from the heart' which sum up what it stands for and what customer needs it will fulfil (e.g. Nando's "pride, passion, courage and family"). In terms of *product elements*, great thought must also go into designing and commissioning the brand's name (will it be, for example, descriptive, alliterative, iconographic, personified, geographic or made up?), logo (visual identifier), tagline (catchphrase), graphics (shapes and patterns), *icons and stories* and so forth. Are they evocative? Do they symbolise what the brand seeks to represent? Will they appeal to core customers (without offending infrequent users)? Do they create feelings of warmth and affection?

- **Provide distinctive and generous benefits** – it is important that the product appears unique to customers, offering benefits that other brands don't. Leaders can achieve clarity in this process by leveraging the product essence to define the distinctive functional and emotional attributes that appeal to tangible and intangible customer requirements. *Functional benefits* can be product-based (quality and consistency) or economic (high perceived value); and *emotional benefits* can be psychological (identity, feeling and aspiration) or sociological (affiliation, community and sociability).

- **Have happy workers** – during the design stage the leader will be focused upon building a compelling concept that has traction in the external market. However, during this process of concept construction (s)he must simultaneously contemplate how the brand will be made salient by being brought alive internally. The functional and emotional benefits that the brand offers for customers must be mirrored by a set of clear benefits for staff that will be energised and come to personify the brand. These will be considered in the following sections of this book.

- **Constantly surprise and delight guests** – although this might sound counterintuitive, products that are loved surprise and delight their customers through under-promising and over-delivering on the overall experience. How? Essentially by giving loyal customers unexpected treats or over-indexing on product quality, service and amenity in relation to price, leading to perceptions from customers that they are getting a really good deal. Also, companies that are able to customise and tailor their products to individual needs and demands are also likely to be received more warmly that those that are 'fixed' and homogenous.

CASE STUDY 5 – **VANESSA HALL, CO-FOUNDER OF JACK & ALICE**

Vanessa co-founded Jack & Alice with her husband Mark in 2015. Jack & Alice is a female-friendly, all-day wine bar and pantry that has (after an extremely successful launch in Gerrards Cross) expanded to three sites, with several more planned. Previously, Vanessa was CEO of YO! Sushi and has run a number of upmarket hospitality brands such as All Bar One, Premium Country Dining Group, Village Pub and Kitchen and Miller and Carter. At the prestigious Casual Dining Restaurant and Pub Awards in 2017, the Jack and Alice brand won both the Independent Casual Dining Restaurant of the Year and the Small Casual Dining Employer of the Year categories.

Mark and I believed that there was a gap in the high-street market – particularly within the Home Counties – for a food and drink concept that catered to 'London tastes' but was more accessible and friendly. We wanted to design an *evocative experience* that would transcend all other offers in its competitive set (coffee houses, bistros, wine bars and pubs), making it the first port of call for discerning females and couples. But fundamentally we wanted to design an all-day experience that both our guests and team would *love*. How did we set about doing this?

- **Stand for something good** – Jack & Alice has a heart in the middle of its branding and this motif is used in key touchpoints throughout its design. It exemplifies what we are all about: *touching people's hearts through our hospitality, design and ambience...*

- **Warm personality** – Jack & Alice are the names of our grandparents, so the concept is founded on a strong notion of family. This ancestral connection informs what we want this brand to personify: sociable, homely, welcoming, feel good... It stands for the important little things in life, an intimate, familiar haven where people can take time out from the madness of life. It is this warm personality that gives our brand a clear identity – a compelling backstory which is built on love, warmth and nostalgic memories...

- **Distinctive and generous benefits** – these apply to both guests and team. Guests are offered a true form of hospitality where charming staff treat them as if they were guests in their own home. They are offered quality food and drink at affordable prices in a comfortable environment that offers a twist on the traditional wine-bar offer. It offers casual indulgence – generous homemade salads, sharing boards, toasties, bakes and treats accompanied by a great wine list. People are welcomed and made to feel at ease in cosy and stylish surroundings. Our team are chosen because they will fit into our family values.

- **Happy workers** – Mark and I are hands on in the business and we try to set the cultural tone, particularly at new openings. Although we might be physically remote, we aim to generate positive feelings and behaviours by the signals we send out on a day-to-day basis. The quality of people Jack & Alice employs, the little gestures we make to recognise good work, empathetic decision making on a regular basis. What we are trying to build here is a family-based culture, where our managers and team imitate and build upon our beliefs and values, which in turn is transmitted to our guests...

- **Surprise and delight guests** – we recently introduced a loyalty card: "friend of Jack" or "friend of Alice". We try and constantly refresh and innovate, often using ideas from the team, ensuring each new opening has evolved from things learned. In an informal way, it is in our nature at Jack & Alice to constantly delight and surprise. Accommodating guests even when we are jam-packed to overflowing! Making social connections and *natural* (as opposed to forced) conversation with our guests. Getting the team to act naturally can be a challenge – it's quite intimidating, being on stage. It is about ensuring that the team understand and absorb the message that Jack & Alice is all about *heartfelt love and warm hospitality*...

CASE STUDY 6 – **CHRIS MOORE, EX-CEO, DOMINO'S PIZZA GROUP**

Chris joined Domino's in its early days, playing a large part in driving its stellar growth from 37 to over 700 stores. Domino's is recognised as one of the most successful and valuable franchised networks in the UK today. Here he reflects one the cornerstones of its success – the emotional intelligence of its leaders.

When I say that successful branded franchises win by having a good *emotional intelligence*, what I mean is their leadership attends to the (more difficult) *'softer' cultural side* of the organisation in order to achieve 'hard' tangible outcomes... what we did at DPG was to produce a culture that was *akin to a club* where good franchisors *loved* the organisation and did the right thing for the greater good. The way in which we created this was with:

- **A warm personality** – people at all levels of the organisation needed to know what we were all about... our company mantra was 'Sell More Pizza, Have More Fun'... simple, quirky, warm, engaging, resonant...

- **Empathy** – when building up the network, we were signing up franchisees for long periods of time and it was important – doubly so when we abandoned owned stores – to have knowledgeable, credible, inspirational leaders with high levels of operational /support expertise and strong franchisee ties. You have to have a system based on long-term relationships. The fact that at one time our leadership team had an average of 13 years' service was incredibly important for information/knowledge continuity purposes... The way in which our leaders 'divided up the profit pig' was also critical... to my mind a proper share that worked for DPG (as a quoted company) was one-third franchisor, two-thirds franchisee: when things were challenging – particularly during food-cost inflation spurts and the subsequent credit crunch in the late noughties – we tried to keep to this split by maintaining product cash profit (at the expense of erosions in net margin).

- **Happy people** – at DPG, in addition to district and regional meetings, we held two major set-piece events which were *deliberately inclusive*... In October every year we had a managers conference where we got them pumped up for Xmas... Our key event was the DPG awards ceremony in March/April where, after having business and information sessions at the beginning, we had a big bash at the end... But the point is this: we didn't only invite franchisees: we also invited their partners (who bear as much, if not more of the burden!) and franchisees invited managers, along with other staff members and drivers that had been nominated for the top awards... the *mood and spirit was phenomenal – it really glued us together for the year...* even some of the franchisees and leadership team joined me in getting dressed up on stage (I made a great Marilyn Monroe and a cracking Queen!) and we made fun of ourselves... We chanted '*Who Are We? Domino's! What Are We? Number One! What Do We Do? Sell More Pizzas, Have More Fun!'...* This 'anglicised Americanism', as I call it, might seem trite to cynics, but it worked: for a few days we were all together... happily celebrating winning... with precious little sense of hierarchy and looking forward to winning together over the next year.

CASE STUDY 7 – **BERRY CASEY, FOUNDER OF HACHÉ**

In 2016, better burger concept Haché was sold for a price premium to a consortium leisure group. Here the founder Berry Casey describes two key ingredients underpinning its success.

We came up with the idea for an upmarket burger restaurant in the mid-noughties. Central to our insights was the need to be differentiated from the competition both in terms of quality and price. But just as important was the culture of the brand required to underpin the brand's personality... so how have we ensured that our service is distinctive?

- **Love** – at Haché (which means 'to chop' in French) our philosophy is "j'aime Haché, j'aime la vie" (love Haché, love life). We are in the business of *making people happy* – both staff and customers. Yes, the core strength of the brand is derived from obsessive attention to detail to the core product (that we don't undermine by 'trading on price') but it is the philosophy that underpins our brand that our competitors can't copy.

- **Happy Team** – our brand is like a family and, as the song goes, "the love you take, is equal to the love you make". A happy team means a happy ambience – we have a very low staff turnover and all our general managers have been promoted from within. The skills and talents of our staff are amazing (most of whom are aged between 18 and 35). They are well-qualified, energetic, positive people who 'get' Haché. Yes, we've had to professionalise and standardise systems as we've grown (taking on more people to support the brand) but we have kept our formula for maintaining team spirit...

Designing an Evocative Experience (generating LOVE) – Five Key Points

- Be distinctive
- Create a soul and personality
- Provide benefits to guests that they can't get elsewhere
- Create a family team, a proud tribe of employees
- Constantly innovate and surprise loyal guests

---

2. ENTICE TALENT – Hire (Generating DESIRE)

The second moment of truth is the hiring of great talent. Service businesses are people businesses – they thrive through attracting staff with great people-handling skills. This means that organisations need to communicate with and attract the right profile of candidates, namely: those with a great attitude and a real service personality. People who actively derive pleasure from the act of helping others have a sunny disposition and really enjoy making others feel happy. Great service companies like South West Airlines hire for attitude because – as their CEO, Herb Kelleher, once said – "we can change skill levels, but we can't change attitudes". Hence South West aim to recruit staff that match their ideal profile as individuals who embrace teamwork, demonstrate altruism, have a self-depreciating demeanour, take their work – but not themselves – too seriously and do what is necessary to help the company reach its goals. But how should they go about achieving this? It is a noble aspiration to wish to entice talent with great emotional intelligence and a high level of service orientation, but competition for such people is stiff. Top service talent is probably already embedded in companies elsewhere. How do you prize them away? The answer lies in overcoming potential recruits' *caution* about transitioning between organisations, stimulating interest through generating genuine *desire* to join your outfit. But how do you get talent to *covet* joining your organisation? What do inspirational leaders do to create real *appetite, hunger and thirst* to get talent to try and hop on board? Our view is that they animate feelings of desire amongst talented people by enticing them: having an appealing brand positioning, acceptable terms and conditions, alluring marketing, rigorous assessment methods and appealing to opinion formers.

- **Appealing brand proposition** – the first building prop that requires putting in place (echoing the observations we made in the section above) is an appealing brand proposition that will create an aura and draw for the right candidates. The perceptions of prospective staff will be influenced by the reputation of the brand: something that they will have felt either through their own dealings with the brand or from what other people say (either directly or online). Their judgements about what the company is like will be disproportionately influenced by what other people think because of how it might affect their so-called 'relative social standing' in relation to their peers (i.e. whether it enhances or degrades their status) and/or the degree to which it bolsters their own levels of identity and feelings of self-esteem. In short: will a direct association with this company make them look and feel good? Considering recent entrants onto the job market (millennials), talent is more likely to gravitate towards companies that espouse values of sustainability and societal wellbeing, rather than those who are purely driven by a singular profit motive.

- **Acceptable terms and conditions** – an attractive brand proposition is vitally important, but this must usually be accompanied by acceptable terms and conditions of employment. Often the two go hand in hand: brands with great reputations have the resources and momentum to fashion great 'employment branding' that complements their 'product branding'. Some organisations consciously strengthen their employment offer (through generous pay rates, incentives, benefits and working condition) to gain competitive advantage for talent within local/national labour markets or – as in the case of the John Lewis Partnership – it is woven into the ownership structure of the company. Other institutions, however, are able to offer terms and conditions that sit beneath market rates because the intrinsically 'worthwhile work' they offer (e.g. the church, the army and charities) transcends extrinsic monetary needs. Such occupations really represent a calling, where employees are willing to make personal sacrifices in order to 'do good'. In light of this insight, we would offer the observation that companies that operate in sectors traditionally regarded as low paying – retail and hospitality especially – should think hard about what the work they offer will *mean* to those that they hope to entice on board. For sure, organisations operating within these sectors must offer competitive terms and conditions to prospective pools of emotional labour, but these will fall short in comparison companies seeking to attract cognitive labour. Organisations within these sectors must think about the 'calling' they are offering potential recruits which offer high levels of intrinsic value, alongside acceptable terms and conditions that fulfil basic extrinsic needs.

- **Alluring marketing** – the way in which an organisation presents itself to potential recruits is, of course, crucial in securing the right calibre of candidates. Often recruitment is left solely to HR professionals, who take traditional approaches to attracting talent: constructing and overseeing standard recruitment advertisement 'templates' that are deployed locally (through job centres and in business units) or online. Their content can be dry and have a poor 'reach' to market, barely standing out from the competition, having an indifferent effect on the behaviours of job seekers. The best recruiters do not limit the task to HR – they also involve the skills of the marketing function, which appreciates the importance of alluring imagery, impactful presentation and demographic targeting. Some companies have 'joined up thinking' between their brand advertising and recruitment campaigns, with – for instance – airline companies using highly 'aesthetic' staff to headline prime campaigns (Virgin, Emirates and British Airways being notable examples). Also, many successful hospitality companies – rather than using blunt, rational job advertisements – take a totally *uncorporate* approach. They show how they value their people by using real-life case studies of the individuals who do the jobs: citing the excitement and satisfaction they derive from doing a job they love in a company they are highly committed to. Their stories – of what they do, their experiences and journey – are the best recruiting sergeants for an organisation. This is because potential recruits (who are very often customers of the brand!) can emotionally engage and identify with beautiful, uplifting stories that imply that, one day, they too could experience similar success. Showing how Jack or Zoe – in their own words – have been nurtured, trained and progressed through the organisation connects with the dreams and aspirations of job seekers, who feel (as all humans do) an overwhelming *desire* for personal improvement, achievement and worthwhile contribution!

- **Rigorous assessment** – once interest has been generated and applications have been made for positions, how do organisations sift and assess the right people? In spite of the usual aspiration to recruit so-called A-grade talent, organisations usually have to shift their sights to recruiting B-graders who have the potential to shift up to A-grade status. (This is due to highly competitive labour markets, the paucity of genuine A-graders and the unwillingness of such people to move, due to the positive experiences and opportunities provided in their current organisations.) So how do you spot these nascent personalities – the people who will be tireless advocates, zealots and evangelists for your brand; those with pace, a pleasing aesthetic appearance, energy and determination to do well for both themselves and the company?

  - *Pre-screen* – usually organisations will pre-screen applications using minimum qualification thresholds and conducting analysis of prior experience. Often this is a paper-based exercise: applicants apply online and their applications and CVs are automatically sifted and scrutinised for progression to the next stage. This lean approach to recruiting is insufficient to capture people's real personality, desires, aspirations and motives for applying for the role. The best companies conduct telephone or video follow ups to dig deeper, attempting to calibrate the true character and potential of the applicant. What do they really feel about the job and the company? What are their dreams and aspirations? How would they fit with the organisation?

○ ***Competency/values-based interviews*** – in order to introduce some rigour into the process, competency or values-based interviews are sometimes used, either at pre-screen or formal interview assessment stage, to establish whether the candidate has certain essential service-based traits such as *energy, optimism, curiosity* and *hope*. This will involve asking how candidates have reacted to or handled challenges and life situations in the past. A technique that we would advocate as being particularly revealing and successful in uncovering people's core values is asking candidates to *list three people that you admire and respect, and explain why*. The traits that they mention are – most likely – indicative of the traits that they aspire to imitate and copy. For instance, those that mention their mother and father – citing their courage, drive, perseverance and unconditional love – have chosen powerful role models that are likely to have a strong predictive effect on their past, present and future behaviours. Those that cite vacuous reality TV stars, who glory in empty self-projection and instant stardom, show themselves up to have (perhaps) delusional fantasies about how 'real' success is achieved.

○ ***Strength-based interviews*** – another way of unearthing a person's true character is to locate what they are really good at rather than merely what they might be capable of doing. This involves uncovering candidate preferences and making a judgement on how these might fit with the organisation's values and culture. Useful questions we have found to unlock strengths and weaknesses include: *can you describe a good day you've had? what do people say you are good at? what makes you really happy at work? what do you find comes easiest to you at work? what sort of experiences give you real energy?* and *tell me about something that you've achieved that you are really proud of?* Answers to these questions will often uncover the dominant profile of candidates: whether or not they are 'balancers' (somebody interested in maintaining a healthy work–life balance), 'careerists' (an ambitious career builder), 'social seekers' (interested in work for purely relational reasons), 'advocates' (an individual who sincerely advances the cause of their organisation) or 'pragmatics' (only interested in work for reward and monetary purposes).

○ *Audition, role play, trials* – of course, particularly for service-based roles, the best way of judging candidate suitability is through analysing people's behaviour with other team members and customers. This can either be achieved through 'theatrical simulated' auditions and role plays or on-the-job trials (with the former, ideally being succeeded by the latter). What one is looking out for here are many of the traits mentioned above plus other ones such as rapport and (in the case of more technical jobs) fine hand-to-eye motor skills. Getting candidates to act out their reactions to certain situations and how they spontaneously handle specific customer requests and problems will give an indication of their 'service orientation'. Trial periods on the job enable co-workers to assess candidates' overall capability and ability to gel with both the team and customers. This is a technique that has proven to be successful for many years for sector-leading companies such as Pret a Manger.

○ *Emotional intelligence testing* – the one thread that runs through this section is the argument that, in service-based environments in particular, companies must concentrate their efforts on hiring people with great service personalities. Furthermore, we suggest that this can be scrutinised and tested by examining prior experience, in-depth focused interviewing and behavioural observation. But we need to expand upon what companies need to look for, given the importance of this characteristic. Essentially, great service companies hire people with high levels of *emotional intelligence*. That is to say, individuals who are able to empathise with their co-workers and customers and are able to put themselves in their shoes. Such people intuitively understanding how others feel at any given moment and in any particular circumstance, and modify their own behaviour accordingly to achieve optimal outcomes from their interactions. There are many ways that companies can test for EI – some of these techniques are outlined above. But there is one technique that trumps all others, namely: testing levels of personal self-awareness and insight.

In his masterful treatise on EI, Daniel Goleman argues that individuals with high levels of EI achieve high levels of personal self-awareness and awareness of others. Furthermore, this high personal awareness leads to high levels of self-control, which in turn leads to a strong awareness of (and potentially control over) others, resulting in good conflict management and superior personal relationships. This ability to read others' feelings and moderate one's behaviour accordingly to effect positive outcomes is rooted, then, in the ability to 'know oneself in order to know others'. This can be tested through interviews and observation, but validity is increased if psychometric testing is included, particularly tests that ask candidates to honestly appraise their feelings and reactions in certain situations. Follow-up interview questions that probe answers to Likert 1-10 (a scale of 'always' to 'never') questions, such as "I never get stressed" or "I am always optimistic", will reveal much about the honesty and self-insight of the prospective candidate. What companies are looking for here is individuals who produce an authentic, balanced account of the strengths and weaknesses of their personality and behaviour. Such people are more likely to be aware of what they need to compensate for in their dealings with other people and, more importantly, what they need to identify in the makeup of the people they are dealing with!

- **Appeal to opinion formers** – in order to entice the right candidates there is another dimension that recruiters must consider – particularly in entry-level jobs for younger candidates - namely: the perceptions of opinion formers such as family and careers advisors. A recent study conducted into the lack of apprenticeships being taken up in the builders' merchant sector in the UK found that one of the main reasons for a lack of draw amongst young people was due to the poor perceptions of the industry held by significant others who advised potential recruits on career choices. The research concluded that for apprenticeship schemes in this sector to become more appealing, the benefits of entering this profession had to be 'sold up the chain' in order to increase the chances of take up. Overall, the authors concluded, the industry itself had to work far harder to convince potential recruits and their advisors of the merits of joining a sector that (contrary to opinion) offers interesting, varied work and huge career opportunities to highly motivated individuals.

Indeed, this is a problem that McDonald's UK confronted and overcame in the early 2000s. At the time, the company was under attack – facing food-chain supply shocks (allegations that its beef was contaminated), accusations that its food was contributing to an obesity epidemic and that its jobs were low-paid, low-status 'McJobs'. Its CEO at the time, Steve Easterbrook, drove a strategy to completely revitalise the company: revitalising the menu, freshening the offer, making the supply chain more transparent and also – crucially – completely revamping its employer branding (in conjunction with the HRD at the time, David Fairhurst). Alongside overhauling its terms and conditions (permitting flexible hours, shift swaps, roving contracts etc.), the company also ramped up its training and development systems, offering staff the opportunity to undertake a suite of nationally accredited courses that would improve their levels of skills and employability. In doing so, the company won a suite of awards, became regularly cited as one the UK's best companies to work for and – as a result – made parents feel that McDonald's was a good company for their sons and daughters to work at.

In summary, enticing people to work for your organisation really comes down to creating strong feelings of *desire* amongst potential candidates. In the service sector, many jobs are perceived as being low-paid, dead-end appointments and this – in a sense – is what can give ambitious organisations a huge competitive advantage. By positioning themselves successfully as a brand, offering acceptable terms and conditions, with attractive marketing, rigorous assessment techniques and a strong appeal to opinion formers, organisations can create a 'hunger to join' amongst the talent they want. We would also offer other insights. First, the message that companies must put out is that they are hiring people *not necessarily for what they have done in the past, but what they are going to achieve in the future*. It is this message that they are in the business of *grooming stars* rather than using people as disposable commodities – weaving a compelling narrative of hope and advancement – that will capture the hearts and minds of potential recruits. Second, companies should always highlight, not just the personal benefits that individuals will reap by joining, but also the wider social upsides of joining an elite, high-performing team that derives a huge degree of satisfaction and fun from what it does. Nando's – one of the most successful brands in the UK at the present time – emphasises the importance of family in all of its recruitment advertising, stressing that the organisation – rather than being some impersonal corporate entity – is a close-knit family unit, thereby implying that people actively look after and out for one another. By projecting a strong, positive tribal identity they sell the prospect of offering people a place of work where they will be more than a number and will be respected for their contribution and nurtured to achieve their full potential.

CASE STUDY 8 – **ADRIAN FRID, OPERATIONS DIRECTOR, CAFFÈ NERO**

Adrian Frid is Operations Director at Caffè Nero, having previously led the roll out of the upmarket steakhouse brand, Miller and Carter. Adrian is a veteran of the food service industry, having worked his way up from unit manager over the course of twenty-five years.

Reflecting back on my time as a leader at Miller and Carter and Nero's, *how* have I created real **desire** to join my team? *what* sort of person of person am I looking for? and *which* methods do I use to recruit them?

- **How do I create a desire to join?**
  - *Great brand experience* – a lot of recruits into M&C and Nero's have been tempted to apply because of the positive experiences they have had with the brand and its people. If your brand has credibility and appeal it makes your job as a recruiter a lot easier.
  - *Paint a compelling picture* – when I interview people I tell them that they can be part of something great! But I am also honest. I tell them about what the reality of getting to our final destination is going to be, that it will be a tough route through. But what I say is this: "you will be part of a team on a mission to achieve something – it might be hard going but we will work as a close knit *family* to get through it, supporting one another through difficulties *but* having *fun* together, enjoying the good times".
  - *Authentic values* – what I have found is that, essentially, people will have a great incentive and desire to join me on the journey if they buy into the *values* of me and the brand. Millennials will only join your operation and stay longer if they feel aligned to your values and goals.
  - *Accelerated development programmes* – millennials also need a clear sense that there will be accelerated progression and you've got to show them how this can happen. Millennials are

a far more promiscuous employment group than previous generations – they will move on quickly if they feel that the brand is not meeting their values and career aspirations.

- o *Security of employment* – for migrants, security of employment and being paid on time is a key motivating factor as they are (particularly in London) paying high rents and surviving hand-to-mouth, initially. They also are attracted to places where fellow migrants from the same or similar backgrounds are established and doing well: they are great recruiting sergeants because they will have friends back home that might be willing to come over and give it a try.

- **What sort of people do I want to recruit?** – I look for people who have a sense of *urgency*... a spark in their eyes. People who can *energise* other people around them. In one-to-one interviews, auditions and trials you can see this personal energy manifest itself and judge whether they will fit with the people around them and the business. So, I look to employ people with energy and *personality*: you can't fake personality and drive. Technical skills I can give them – it is that get up and go I am looking for!

- **Which methods do we use to get the best people?** – this is the hardest thing, given the explosion in food service brands and the war for talent on the ground. At middle-management level, a lot of people get recruitment agents to do all their work which can be a little frustrating. Also many recruitment companies seem to be pretty lazy scouting talent – just using LinkedIn or Facebook to search for the right candidates. At shop level, great candidates will just 'walk the food service strip' in towns and cities with 50 CVs, so you've got to turn them around quickly. Also you have to have a great online portal where you sift for talent and respond quickly. Speed and a quick turnaround are key otherwise you will lose talent to the competition. So what I would say is this – we have used a multi-channel approach to get the best, but in the end it isn't all down to your processes. Great people will *seek you out* if you have a great brand reputation!

> **Enticing Talent (generating DESIRE) – Seven Key Points**
>
> - Offer worthwhile work
> - Look for service personalities with great attitudes
> - Take an uncorporate marketing approach to hiring
> - Offer terms and conditions that exceed the market•
> - Win over opinion formers (parents, peers etc.)
> - Assess values by asking "who do you respect and why?"
> - Make it clear that you want to 'groom stars'

3. ENTHRAL HEARTS AND MINDS – Onboard (Generating AWE)

The third moment of truth is the onboarding or induction of the talent that has been enticed into the company. It is often said that 'first impressions leave lasting impressions'. Expectations have been raised for candidates during a rigorous selection process and it is crucial that companies, at the very least, overcome any feelings of *scepticism* by meeting these expectations and deliver on their previous promises or – ideally – wow new joiners by exceeding pre-set expectations. Often induction processes in service-based companies are derisorily short, lacking in both breadth and depth. Due to staff shortages and a lack of resources (training budgets, management time, proper onboarding processes and facilities), new recruits are immediately flung into the frontline with a minimum of training and guidance, where they either sink or swim in a chaotic, disorderly environment. The results of this are extremely costly to companies in terms of both productivity and stability levels. In such contexts new recruits will take a long time to master their role, possibly derailing service delivery and making costly mistakes during their initial stages of employment.

Also, due the pressures and stresses of operating in 'over-sold' jobs, a fair proportion of new recruits will opt to bail out early on, leading to high levels of early-recruit turnover at service-provider level, wasting all the time, money and effort that has gone into recruiting them in the first place. Great service companies do not let this happen. They place an inordinate amount of resource into sympathetically and effectively onboarding new joiners, recognising the immense benefits that can be accrued from placing a disproportionate emphasis on providing quality familiarisation programmes to new recruits. They recognise that *socialising, integrating and providing essential skills* early on pays dividends for individuals, teams and the organisation in the longer term. What they essentially do is inculcate feelings of *awe* amongst new joiners through the way in which they treat them within this early career stage. A deep feeling amongst new joiners that – due to their initial experiences – they have indeed accomplished something significant by joining this *impressive* organisation. So how do high-performing service organisations engender these feelings of wonder and pride amongst new starters? How do they integrate them into their culture quickly, ensuring that they act in accordance to the prevailing norms, customs and values of the organisation? How do they ensure – from the get go – that their *hearts and minds are enthralled* by what they initially experience in their early days? Our view is that they instil feelings of pride and enthral new recruits by providing a warm welcome, deep immersion, inspiring 'why, where and how', underpinned by heart-warming stories, legends and icons of the organisation.

- **Warm welcome** – the first thing that organisations must ensure is that new recruits are given a heartfelt warm welcome to the company. Some organisations – due to their large numbers of recruits (especially through expansion drives) – will be able to do this in an orchestrated set-piece manner, involving senior leaders, on the first day of a four-to-six-week structured familiarisation programme. This will not be possible in many contexts because – due to waxing and waning resourcing requirements – new joiners don't onboard simultaneously. But the same philosophy should apply. On day one, the new recruit must be fulsomely and warmly welcomed into the company by somebody in a position of responsibility (whether locally or centrally). Also – if possible – the new recruit should be 'buddied up' with an experienced co-worker and/or assigned a suitable mentor straight away. This will give new joiners an immediate sounding board, confidante and source of instruction. Remember, most new recruits start off eagerly wishing to prove themselves but are conscious that they do not know 'how things are really done around here'. This anxiety can be removed immediately by conjoining them with old hands who know the ropes.

- **Deep immersion** – in addition to this warm welcome and the provision of a buddy or mentor to ensure new joiners feel cared for, an intensive immersion programme should be triggered to integrate individuals into the ethos and ways of working of the organisation. In terms of understanding ways of working, two dimensions will be covered: an appreciation of organisational strategy/structure/ processes and an understanding of the job role itself. In terms of the former, it is essential that new recruits gain understanding how all the 'parts fit together' and 'how to get things done around here'. Understanding how their unit and job fits into the corporate whole is important not only for information purposes, but also to prevent a silo mentality occurring amongst new joiners. That is to say, a One Team Approach means considering the whole corporate entity, rather than just their own domain – respecting the contribution of others is a core tenet that must be taken on board as soon as possible in the joining process.

In terms of the second of our two dimensions – the job itself – essential skills must be implanted in the initial period (not least technical and legal) in order to fulfil statutory obligations and the safety of customers. A further section will deal with training systems and the critical role they play in augmenting service skills and giving individuals feelings of confidence to transition successfully through their trial/probationary periods – but in these initial stages at least, the minimum technical skills must be implanted within individuals to ensure the company is acting safely and legally. Without this, its reputation could be placed in severe jeopardy. Getting back to the ideal length and content of immersion programmes, Ritz Carlton – an exemplar of induction training within the hospitality sector – has beacon units of excellence where they thoroughly induct new recruits, showcasing all the different functions, strategy and policies of the company and its core service philosophy ("we are ladies and gentlemen serving ladies and gentlemen"). They follow up this immersion with a six-hour catch up which they term 'DAY 21', in which the GM of their new unit conducts the first hour, asking: how have you found your experience so far? What did we miss out? How can we improve the induction process? Indeed, it is this focus on quality and continuous improvement that sets Ritz Carlton apart from its peers.

- **Inspiring 'why and how'** – reference was made above to inculcating the ethos of the organisation into new recruits. Obviously, new entrants into the organisation will have a fairly clear perception of what the core philosophy and strategy of the organisation is due to their prior research and interactions with the firm throughout the recruitment process. But now the rubber will hit the road! What is it really like within the organisation and what is its DNA? New recruits will be influenced by the authentic manner in which people around them act – do they actually live and convey the organisation's 'noble purpose' and 'compelling values' on a daily basis?

- ○ ***Noble purpose*** – as we have previously said, many talented recruits will be drawn to organisations because of what they stand for and the 'calling' they provide. Once they have entered the portals, however, companies must reiterate to their new recruits why they exist. This is usually done casually and badly, through impersonal classroom tuition or manuals. Done well, it is usually most powerfully conveyed by senior leaders, line managers and co-workers who exemplify, believe in and live the purpose of the organisation. For instance, Pizza Hut UK – an organisation that has been dramatically revived under its CEO, Jens Hofma, in recent times (it grew its enterprise value from £1 to nearly £250m from 2011–16) – crafted a noble purpose within Hofma's team that resonates powerfully throughout his whole organisation:

  > we are fuelled by the passion that '**we are doing good**'… we are giving people a social experience for £10 per head that they wouldn't get elsewhere… we are honoured to have their hard earned cash and are proud that we are giving people value and a great experience… nobody else does what we do in our segment of the market… we make our staff proud of this!

  This passionate belief in in 'doing good' has given Jens and his team a feeling of real pride and self-esteem – something that has undoubtedly contributed to the resurgence of the organisation in recent times.

- ○ ***Compelling values*** – organisations can have a noble purpose which explains *why* it exists, but *how* do they make sure this is behaviourally underpinned? The answer is that they have a clear code of values that prescribe intentional, permissible and acceptable behaviours that will deliver their purpose. Zappos, the successful US online shoe retailer founded in 1999, had a singular start-up purpose: to provide the "best selection and best service" to its online customers. This purpose was supported by 10 core values:

1. Deliver WOW through service
2. Embrace and drive change
3. Create FUN and a little weirdness
4. Be adventurous, creative and open-minded
5. Pursue growth and learning
6. Build open and honest relationships through communications
7. Build a positive team and family spirit
8. Do more with less
9. Be passionate and determined
10. Be humble

Zappos' success was such that in 2009 it was purchased by Amazon for $1.2bn; but ever since, it has been maintained as a successful independent entity within the Amazon empire. In the UK, the David Lloyd Leisure Group has transitioned successfully through a few owners whilst steadfastly maintaining market leadership in the midscale health-club segment by staying true to its purpose of making its members "feel special, understood and valued". The five supporting behaviours they expect staff to display – enthusiastic, engaging, expert, empathetic, enabling – are designed to reinforce and strengthen this aim. The point is this: companies that have carefully thought about whether or not their purpose has a worthwhile resonance (to both staff and customers), supplemented by purposeful, aligned values that shape the required behaviours to bring it to fruition on a daily basis, are far more likely to achieve enduring success than those that don't. As trite as it may seem, carefully crafted purpose and values count; they give real *meaning* to individual employees' endeavours. Humans want to engage in work that is worthwhile, with co-workers that act in collegiate, helpful ways with a happy demeanour. New recruits will sense almost immediately whether what they have been 'told and sold' during their selection process is rhetoric or reality: if it is the former, they are likely to be disappointed and demotivated; if it is the latter, they will be inspired and motivated to fulfil the overarching needs of the organisation and ensure their customers have a great experience.

- **Heart-warming stories, legends, symbols and icons** – another thing that great service companies do to penetrate the hearts and minds of new recruits is stir feelings by evoking positive imagery in powerful stories: recalling legendary figures/events and drawing attention to symbols and icons that are crucial manifestations of the company's heritage and DNA. This is something that Nando's, the UK's premier fast casual dining restaurant chain, is particularly good at.

How It All Began – The Nando's Story

The Nando's story started centuries ago, when the Portuguese explorers set sail for the East in search of adventure and the legendary spice route. The winds of Africa called them ashore and it was there, under the warm sun, in the rich soil that they discovered the African Bird's Eye Chilli or PERi-PERi. A spice like no other, they used it to create a unique sauce that put fire in their bellies and ignited passion in their souls. A few hundred years later (in 1987 to be exact), it was the same PERi-PERi sauce that inspired Fernando Duarte to invite his friend Robbie Brozin to a humble Portuguese eatery in the heart of Rosettenville, South Africa to try some mouth-watering PERi-PERi marinated and basted chicken. It wasn't just the best chicken Robbie had ever tasted: it was love at first bite! The rest, as they say, is history. Today, you can find Nando's restaurants, our addictive sauces and tasty grocery range right around the world. Whether you're a first-time visitor or an old friend, we can't wait to welcome you and serve you a delicious fix of PERi-PERi!

In this story, Nando's highlights the legends, symbols and icons that underpin the brand. Through storytelling, they seek to emphasise the provenance and authenticity of the brand, the fearless determination of their founding fathers and their mission to spread Nando's happiness around the world. Its evocative and romantic narrative is designed to intrigue and inspire both customers and staff alike. The raging success of the brand in the UK bears testament to the fact that – gilded or not – the company has woven a powerful story that captures hearts and minds. The success of the brand and the pride that staff members feel in being part of the famous Nando's family have been recognised in several national staff engagement awards. It is also a matter of public record that Nando's has one of the lowest staff turnovers in the UK food-service industry (19 per cent versus an industry average of 61 per cent), signalling that when people join, a magical spell is cast over them and they stay for an average of five years or more.

In summary, once great service companies have got new recruits through their doors, they work hard to engender instant feeling of *awe* that they have accomplished joining something of *significance* – rather than feelings of despondency and disillusionment that they have made a catastrophic mistake signing up to a fabricated entity. Too often companies take a lackadaisical approach to onboarding new employees, many regarding them as dispensable cannon fodder, perversely reasoning that – because most of their new joiners are likely to leave early – they shouldn't make any tangible effort to integrate them into, and familiarise them with, the wider organisation. This 'lean' (mean!) approach to induction is a false economy which can have disastrous ramifications. Transient, uncaring staff who provide poor levels of service will ultimately cost the organisation goodwill, customers and sales. As this section has argued, great service companies enthral the hearts and minds of 'newbies' by providing them with a warm welcome followed by a deep immersion. Such companies bring their noble purpose and compelling values alive through the behaviours of the people new employees initially meet and the heart-warming stories, legends, symbols and icons that they learn about more fully as they begin their eagerly anticipated career journeys.

CASE STUDY 9 – **DAVID SINGLETON, VICE PRESIDENT HOSPITALITY, AL TAYER GROUP**

David Singleton is the Vice President, Hospitality at the Al Tayer Group based in Dubai. His arm of the business runs 11 brands in a variety of locations. Al Tayer is long-established, successful family business based in the United Arab Emirates that specialises in running luxury fashion and automotive retail businesses in 'high-end' locations across the Middle East. David previously held senior hospitality posts in Russia and UK with a number of industry-leading brands.

How do you onboard people successfully? To my mind you do three things well: first, *you recruit for values* (so that the right person–brand fit occurs from day one); second, you *systematically immerse* newbies in a professional, pre-planned manner; and third, you *capture their hearts* by how you really treat them once they are inside the organisation.

- **Recruit for values** – we often find ourselves talking about the importance of recruiting and the concept of the 'attraction game' that never ages. How do you attract, recruit and retain the best possible people? When in the operational line, I always used to respond to those who said they could never recruit like this: "you have one branded unit, don't tell me you can't find 10 or 20 like-minded fabulous personalities that you can train to serve, pour beer or learn to cook!" You have to place engaging managers at the helm who recruit people *just like them* to grow. They need to be people who were *socially aligned to the business* (so you'd market vacancies amongst your best customers), those who **loved** the place and weren't afraid of working hard. **Never, ever, ever, never compromise your recruitment values.** The minute you do is the minute your good people start to doubt you and question your judgement as an inspirational good leader. Team dynamics will started to crack and you put your earning potential at risk. Good people want to work with good people; in fact, they thrive together. Never make it hard for them. They will always find another place to work if you give them reason to leave (such as working with idiots!).
- **Systematically immerse** – in Al Tayer, we onboard on the same day of the week, regardless of position. Everyone has an onboarding

pack ahead of time, which includes a full induction folder, *where* to meet, *who* to meet and at *what* time they should be there. The first few days are taken up with members of *every* part of the business who will come and see the new cohort and explain the role of the business, from audit to each commercial stream, beauty, luxury fashion, hospitality and so on. This will be led by a senior trainer, or ops manager within the businesses. One of the days will be spent in a mall where new recruits will have a tour and see the wide range of brands Al Tayer represents. Once corporate induction is complete, they head off to their appropriate training channels. When new recruits arrive in emerging markets such as the UAE, they are invariably green, unlike more mature markets that we might be more used to. They may not have had the luxury of growing up around cafes and restaurants that we take for granted and as a result their welcome experience can be **awe-inspiring** and overwhelming for many of them. The onboarding process is critical, and not only is basic product knowledge an essential part of the training, but consider etiquette, cultural, governance training as well as organisational training. It's so important to set clear expectations during induction period – both ways. Why should we just set high expectations of them? Employees should know what to expect of us as leaders and mentors making a disciplined, set probation clear and straightforward with no surprises. This training *should* be no different to that for the more mature markets many of us are more used to, but we often forget it's importance and work hard to get them to work quickly without realising the potential productivity compromise. In my experience in the Middle East, new colleagues we bring in from overseas are sponges for knowledge relishing the new opportunity that they have to grow and it is a genuine pleasure to work with them!

- **Capture hearts** – but at the end of the day, it's the way we treat people that counts. At Al Tayer we have strong core values focused on delighting customers, respecting our community, plus (and this is the starting point!) caring for and empowering our employees. When we are hand-picking and bringing people on board to work for us from destinations such as Egypt, Pakistan, the Philippines and India, we are taking them far away from their families and homeland. The thousands of people who have made this journey work exceptionally hard to send money back to their extended families, and quite often to support young children they have left at home. We *care* for our colleagues in many ways, but always bringing them into the heart of the brand they are working with, making them feel special and part of it. We want them to be truly proud of their work place and do all we can to make sure this *emotional investment* carries forward to the 'last three feet'. In my area of the business we have industry-leading retention, NPS and employee satisfaction scores mainly, I believe, because of the focus we place on *caring for staff*. My leadership style has always been about maintaining and demanding the highest standards – but repaying that through *emotional investment*. Leadership is about doing little things that mean a *big* deal to other people. It is about investing *emotional energy* in people so that, in the end, you have captured their hearts, their trust and their commitment. As a leadership team we often use the phrase '*people before numbers*'. This can be challenging for many businesses given their commercial focus on satisfying a constant demand for improved efficiencies, but we really do place a high focus on our people. It's not just important, it's a priority. In January 2016, I learned that one of my (identified) future leaders had just returned from the Philippines to take his second child back to live with his mother until he could afford for his family to live in Dubai, due to the high cost of living. As a team, we engaged our HR resources to ensure we fast tracked his training, development and subsequent promotion to a point where he could afford for them to live together. One year later they were reunited and Caffè Nero UAE now has one of the most motivated international brand champions we could ever have wished for. He regards his UAE team as his extended family and in the spirit of 'pay it forward', the brand and wider business continues to benefit...

Enthral Hearts and Minds (generating AWE) – Six Key Points

- Warm welcome on day one
- Surround newbies with helpful teamers who live the values
- Immerse newbies in all vital aspects
- Articulate the business's 'noble purpose'
- Heart-warming stories of heroes, icons and legends
- 'Check Back' for understanding and feelings

4. EQUIP SKILLS – Train (Generating CONFIDENCE)

The fourth moment of truth is equipping staff with key skills to do their jobs. The *right* people with the *right* attitudes have been inducted into the company and fitted with the *right* roles but the organisation must reinforce and enhance skills individuals already have or fill in the gaps that exist in their level of capability. Too often new hires are not only selected on the basis of cursory levels of assessment and induction but are also thrown into the frontline with only basic health and safety compliance training (designed purely to protect the company from potential legal action). Why is this so? The primary reason relates to cost. Training is viewed as an expensive process, a visible cost that can be pared back in order to inflate profitability. Secondly, senior managers are often sceptical about its net benefits. Proving a hard ROI and return on training investment is highly difficult and something that HR professionals, in particular, often fail to achieve. Thus, when the P&L is being scrutinised at senior levels within organisations, training – regarded as a 'soft intangible' cost rather than a 'hard tangible' benefit – is often a place where the 'axe is wielded' in order to 'hit the numbers'.

This is a false economy. Imagine a top-flight football team suspending all training because it is too expensive, expecting its players to turn up on a Saturday and perform on the pitch against well-prepared opposition! The reality is that truly great organisations spend a disproportionate amount of their time, energy and money on training their employees (both newbies and existing) in order to ensure quality, consistency and stability. That is say they do so to safeguard the quality of their product, their consistency/accuracy of delivery and retention/stability of their workforce. The latter point is key. Training promotes not only higher levels of competence amongst team members but also increased feelings of *confidence* amongst individuals that they are capable of fulfilling the requirements of both the company and their customers. Making team members feel less exposed and ***vulnerable*** – more optimistic about their capabilities! – adds boldness to their endeavours, unleashing higher levels of productivity, pace and passion. So what do organisations focus upon to equip their people with skills that grant them real ***confidence*** expediting their roles? Our view is that they do so through defining *clear roles* and responsibilities, inculcating technical skills for *quality*, behavioural skills for *EQ* and cognitive skills for *problem-solving* purposes, encouraging *line manager and co-worker training delivery* and placing a heavy emphasis on *rewarding and accrediting* essential training.

- **Clear role, rights and responsibilities** – as obvious as it might seem, the foundation stone for equipping people with the right skills is the clear delineation of roles, rights and responsibilities. Companies that do this can then match up and design appropriate training packages and programmes that will enable individuals to execute their jobs effectively. Organisations that do this well do a number of things to ensure precision and impact. *First*, job descriptions for roles are written in plain English, isolate the core elements of the role and are treated as a live document – updated on a regular basis to account for changes in the product delivery or customer need. *Second*, an overarching objective to the role (e.g. "to keep customers safe and happy so that they come back time and again") is critical, enabling staff to default to certain behaviours whenever they are in doubt as to which course of action to take. *Third*, companies must ensure that staff are not only told what is expected of them but also *how the company intends to support them* (through resources, facilities, equipment, employment rights, training and incentives). This way, job descriptions are perceived as 'two-way' rather than 'one-way' contracts, more likely to gain worker buy-in and commitment. *Fourth*, it is important that whilst vital tasks are prescribed as clearly as possible, people are made aware that they have an *overriding responsibility to their wider team* and organisation. At times they will be expected (within reason) to adopt a one-team approach and do whatever is asked of them in order to ensure the smooth continuity of the operation. Organisations with rigid job descriptions, strong job demarcations and an aversion to multi-skilling are inflexible and unresponsive. The best organisations make it perfectly clear from day one that, although people have been hired for specific roles, they might – due to changing or unforeseen circumstances – be asked to fulfil reasonable management requests to step up, step across or step into other positions for a time.

- **Technical skills for quality** – buttressing this definition of the role are a series of technical skills programmes aimed at ensuring individuals deliver a *quality* product. Instilling a right-first-time mentality within organisations is essential but people must be given the right skills to expedite their roles effectively. The essential skills for each role will be different: in food-service hospitality organisations, for instance, there will be differing skill requirement sets for front of house, back of house and functional roles. The point is this. There will be specific *practices, processes, policies and procedures* that pertain to the basic expedition of each role – these have to be trained in and re-tested on a regular basis, even when job-holders claim (or protest) that they have the insight and capabilities to do the job. We will deal with who should do the training later on in this section (preferably line managers or co-workers) but it suffices to say that the most effective technical training takes place when people – rather than sitting in a classroom studying theory – can *practically* 'watch, do and review' to enhance their skills. Regular retesting, re-accreditation and certification to practice (see below) also ensures that team members regularly 're-sharpen their saws' and the organisation has the ability to ratchet up the pace during peak trading periods.

- **Behavioural skills for EQ** – great service organisations recruit personnel on the basis of their attitude and levels of service orientation. Companies like Apple, First Direct and John Lewis will then augment these traits with specific habits and approaches. For instance, Apple trains team members in its Apple Stores using 'essential steps of service' which include:

    #1 Approach customers with a personalised warm welcome
    #2 Probe politely to understand all the customer's needs
    #3 Present a solution for the customer to take home today
    #4 Listen for and resolve any issues or concerns
    #5 End with a fond farewell and an invitation to return…

What is telling about these steps of service is the inclusion of words for service behaviours designed to elicit positive feelings and a high degree of emotional customer attachment, such as 'warm', 'polite' and 'fond'. Likewise, First Direct makes its explicit aim to create a 'magical rapport' with its customers, whilst all staff at John Lewis are given training in 'exceptional service encounters'. But what mechanisms do such organisations deploy to actually train for heightened EQ during service interactions? Whether through a mixture of classroom instruction, simulated role play, observed assessment – EQ interventions that have proved particularly successful include:

o ***Evocative guest story telling*** – in order to get staff to gain an appreciation for their customers, staff can do exercises in which they explore the lives of their customers. Who are they? What are their hopes, feelings and aspirations? What is the reality of the daily routine of their home and working life? Understanding this deep context will enable service providers to identify the stresses and strains their customers are exposed to and the search for relief that they seek. After all, most successful companies are in the business of providing products that solve distinctive customer problems (or needs). Taking hospitality as an example, staff benefit hugely from imagining the story behind a family dining-party photograph: that the father is anxious about his job, his wife has had a health scare, the teenage kids are experiencing rebellious growing pains and they have limited disposable income. It is this human scenario that will resonate with staff and enable them to digest why they are 'honour bound' to create a great experience for these customers. In short, they have a duty to give them a good time!

o ***Non-verbal communications training*** – in environments where organisations are providing face-to-face service, spending time on training customer 'non-verbal signalling' will also pay dividends towards increasing EQ skills amongst service personnel. What signals are customers throwing off in terms of their facial expression, posture, appearance, walk and so on? What do these non-verbal communications convey – happiness, desire, sadness, disgust or contempt? What is the dynamic climate? What is the customer there for? What approach would they prefer? Non-verbal training will enable service providers to explore some of these issues and prepare themselves to meld their approaches accordingly – preferably, as the Apple training above suggests, by probing service providers to ask questions and establish requirements before embarking on a set-piece 'sales patter'.

o ***Customer competency training*** – additionally, staff will also benefit from training that alerts and educates them about the levels of customer competency they will be exposed to during service encounters. At first glance this might seem analogous with guest story telling (see above), but such training possesses a subtle twist. Rather than focusing on the backstory of individuals and groups of customers, customer competency training delves into culture and socio-demographic profile. Staff are taught to appreciate the different expectations of customers which are shaped through custom, habit and prior socialisation. Obviously this must be carried out sensitively and professionally, avoiding negative racial and class-based stereotyping. However, staff must be trained to learn that – broadly – different cultural and socio-demographic groups will have different needs and expectations during service encounters (especially where different groups might coalesce and clash!). For instance, customers who hail from cultures with high levels of self-protective leadership, wide power distance and low levels of emancipation are far more likely to take a master–servant approach to their relationship with service providers. Individuals from privileged socio-economic groups are also likely to have high service expectations – particularly in premium contexts – where they are paying for a 'high-end' experience. Lower socio-economic groups who lack power in their daily lives might also act in a 'sovereign' manner during service encounters, because it is the one opportunity they have to exert some influence. As a result of these insights service providers should be trained to keep their cool during difficult – often hostile, rude and aggressive – behaviour from customers, armed with coping mechanisms that help them navigate testing interactions. Also, service providers must be sensitised to the fact that in a modern digital world where trends such as immediacy, impatience, sovereignty, customisation and promiscuity are growing features of customer behaviour, they must adapt their approaches and mindsets accordingly.

o **_Service provider mood training_** –developing the preceding point, most organisations proclaim the primacy of the customer: their fundamental objective being to 'satisfy and delight our customers'. Given the harsh reality of many service encounters, where customers can be ultra-demanding, staff have to be trained not only how to ameliorate complaints (through instant no-quibble rectification, for instance) but also how to manage their own mood and mindset. Customer hostility has a depressing effect on service provider mindsets. Staff may feel angry, frustrated and disgusted at the way they have been treated, lapsing into negative moods – where their own behaviour begins to exacerbate the situation (through displays of deliberate resistance and sabotage!). Service providers must be trained not only to identify the typologies of customer behaviour they face and what they should do to placate, sooth and satisfy but also how to process *their own* feelings. Service providers should be taught that – very often – demanding customer behaviour is not necessarily directed at them per se, rather they are lightning rods for customers to vent their spleen for a variety of complex reasons. Staff should be taught to remain calm and composed in order to defuse situations and not take umbrage at the worst excesses of customer behaviour – the origins of which (often) lie outside their main orbit of control.

- **Cognitive thinking and planning skills** – alongside technical and behavioural interventions, organisations should also look at training mechanisms that improve employee cognitive thinking and planning skills. What is this? Essentially, it is training in problem solving, prioritisation, decision making and time management. Why is it important? The ability to organise one's work and make the correct calls increases capacity and productivity for individuals. It was Flaubert who said "be regular and orderly in your life, so that you may be violent and original in your work!" Too often, organisations neglect this area of training which they assume has been imparted (presumably through osmosis) from line management instruction or prior learning. But training people to process information, prioritise tasks and make decisions that are in the best interests of the team and customer is time well spent. Companies regularly report that millennials (i.e. those born after 1995) coming into the workforce lack these basic skills. Organisations that can provide them – quickly – will benefit from a workforce that has the ability to adjust to and overcome multi-faceted challenges on a day-to-day basis.

- **Line and co-worker delivery** – in addition, the content of training programmes (covering technical, behavioural and cognitive dimensions) organisations must also examine the delivery processes that they have in place. We suggest that companies that get their managers to train and coach their sub-ordinates and co-workers are far more successful and resilient than those that don't. For instance

Pret a Manger's shops all have trainers within their core staff and Ritz Carlton identifies its top performers across its 35 departments whom it deploys as trainers/coaches in their area of expertise. Why is this important? First, it is a well-known adage that 'you learn as you teach' – therefore, those doing the teaching are strengthening their knowledge of their own domain. Second, the credibility of the teaching is enhanced by the fact that it is being delivered by people with deep tacit knowledge, those who 'do it' on a day-to-day basis. Third, it creates a training culture within organisations, where training is not outsourced to a remote training department but is regarded as 'the way that we do things around here'.

- **Prized accreditation awards** – it is one thing equipping individuals with the skills and competencies to increase their confidence and the pace of operations, but how do you make it worthwhile and magical? How do you make training highly prized and sought after? The answer is through attaching meaningful accreditation awards to programmes and modules that individuals – once they have achieved them – can show off to their co-workers, families and friends, thereby increasing their levels of confidence and self-esteem. Intelligent organisations don't just take a 'sheep dip' approach to training, they treat it as a gift they are bestowing upon participants – something that is meaningful and makes the recipients feel proud. In TGI Friday's, as Karen Forester recalled, re-instituting a much-loved certification system for team members had a profound effect:

> When I arrived I could see that the team felt unloved: for instance, the previous owner had dumbed down the uniform, taking away the iconic 'stripes' that recognised outstanding service performance… our teamers kept saying to me "bring back the stripes!"… Symbolically, I re-instituted them in 2009 through a programme called 'Earn Your Stripes' where teamers had to achieve certification… then were recognised at graduation awards ceremonies… For me this marked the symbolic rebirth of the company and was the start of the turnaround… It restored a sense of team aspiration and buzz which translated into providing far better emotional service and higher sales/profits… The hockey stick of our revival definitely started here!

In summary, equipping people with skills will lead to higher levels of *self-confidence* both amongst team members (who feel that they are equipped with the wherewithal to expedite what has been asked of them) and management (who can be more certain that the organisational capability exists to deliver on its promises to customers). Too often, sadly, this confidence is lacking among both cadres of employee. Staff learn on the job and survive or struggle on the frontline and perish. Senior management might delude itself that a 'lean' training strategy will enable them to get by, but business intelligence on quality breakdowns and product inconsistency will demonstrate otherwise. Successful service companies often spend far more money on training than on PR and marketing, recognising that their staff – as the personification of their operations – are the best advertisements and living embodiment of their brands. Distinctive technical, behavioural and cognitive training delivered by line managers and rewarded with meaningful accreditation will provide role clarity and allow organisations to equip themselves with optimal levels of capability. Furthermore, we would argue that companies that go even further, letting their staff increase their product knowledge through 'smelling the sizzle' and shopping the organisation as a customer themselves, add to the insight and capability of their staff. So, having the best-trained staff is a source of competitive advantage for an organisation: particularly when they are also well led, remunerated, communicated with and incentivised – as successive sections will now show.

CASE STUDY 10 – SEAN WHEELER, DIRECTOR OF PEOPLE, PRINCIPAL HOTELS (EX-DORCHESTER COLLECTION AND MALMAISON)

Having enjoyed a lengthy senior HR career in hotels and hospitality, Sean currently leads the People function at Principal, a fast-growing premium city-centre hotel collection that rejuvenates landmark buildings in exceptional locations. Previously Sean was a director of HR at the Dorchester Collection and Group Director of People at Malmaison. Earlier on in his career, he was Head of Training and Director of Operations at TGI Friday's.

How do you instil *confidence* in new joiners, effectively embedding *technical*, *behavioural* and *cognitive* skills? Also, how do you use *co-workers and the line* as a training resource and recognise and *celebrate* training achievement? I shall illustrate how this can be done by using Principal as a direct example.

- **Instilling confidence** – when new people join (especially millennials and migrants) you instil a sense of confidence by showing them that there is a *plan* for them. This reassures them that they are not just being thrown in at the deep end. Millennials, in particular, want to acquire knowledge and develop but they need a defined structure. At Principal we aim to give everyone the best start we can; and this will involve giving them a structured programme for the first three months with both on-the-job and off-the-job training.

- **Technical training for quality** – we take new joiners through the whole service journey. We establish the basics by outlining to them the desired service levels we are trying to achieve. In many ways, when setting up training systems for a relatively new company like Principal, I draw from Friday's experience of 20 or more years ago! Induction is structured at departmental level, where newbies are assigned to buddy coaches and trainers. They have a workbook which is signed off (each time training has been given and the correct behaviours observed) over the first three months. Today a lot of the transactional training can be completed online: health and safety, fire and hazard, food safety, certain elements of customer service and so forth. But much of the training is still done 'hands on', where people 'follow, shadow and show'. Four and eight weeks in we review progress: we also monitor ROI outcomes at three, six and nine months, checking levels of retention and productivity against relative investment.

- **Behavioural training for EI** – behavioural training starts at the beginning. We assess attitude and behaviours against our five main values:
  - *Distinctive* – we aim to stand out from the crowd
  - *Warm* – we care about our guests and one another
  - *Intuitive* – we understand and respond to our guests' needs, feelings and aspirations
  - *Generous* – we are generous with our time and constantly seek to delight and surprise our guests
  - *Local* – we are proud of our location and we know our local area well.

We establish whether or not people fit these values on our Talent Recruitment Days by getting them to complete practical exercises such as 'blind' cocktail making and designing a menu where we can look out for participants' levels of cool headedness, intuition and fun personality. Also, having inducted newbies into the company, we constantly recognise and reinforce good behaviours by rewarding them for doing it right rather than punishing them for getting it wrong! Mystery customer scores will also tell us whether our people are displaying the right behaviours. In the end, in spite of all the effort we have put into training and moulding the right behaviours, if some people fall short, we will inevitably have to part company.

- **Cognitive thinking skills** – we actively train our people to think for themselves by allowing 'freedom within a set frame'. We want the person at source to solve issues rather than going up the hierarchy – which will ultimately lead to delay, frustration and greater cost. So we like to set the parameters, tell people what these are and let them get on with it. We have put together a training module that is helping spread this philosophy throughout our company. We are trying to rid people of the fear of making the wrong decisions. Where mistakes occur (for instance, comping a night's stay rather than offering other 'high-value' items), we will correct through teaching and training rather than punishment and sanctions.

- **Co- and line-worker training** – I am a great believer in training being held at departmental level by highly competent line trainers, with excellent technical and behavioural skills. At present we are actively recruiting internally for departmental coaches who will undergo thorough assessment and training. We are also looking at incentivising and bonusing them relative to a number of KPIs (such as new starter sign-offs after three months, new starter retention rates, sales and average spend per head and mystery customer results). We did it at the Dorchester and it worked particularly well there!

- **Accreditation and celebration** – if newbies pass their three month induction training they are invited to a graduation where they are given a certificate and a free stay with a friend or partner in any of our hotels. It's a big deal and we make it a big landmark occasion. In addition, we have instant recognition 'spotlight cards' that managers can hand out to team members who are 'caught' bringing our values to life, which they are able to redeem for a prize from the people team. We also have awards for quality winners, FOH/BOH employee of the month, apprenticeship completions etc.

CASE STUDY 11 – **LEADER REFLECTIONS ON TRAINING FOR CONFIDENCE (INNVENTURE, LOUNGERS AND BURBERRY)**

Chris Gerrard, Founder, Innventure
On Technical and Behavioural Training

We concentrate on what we call hygiene and relationship training:

- **Technical 'Hygiene Training'** – During induction our staff are trained in the basics (safe/secure, service steps, plate management, order taking/delivery etc.), essentially giving them **confidence** as to what a good job looks like and how this is measured.

- **Emotional 'Relationship Training'** – We work really hard to create an ambition, a vision, within our service providers, by describing what the key 'moments of truth' are for our customers and how these are personally realised by the individual team member. We explain to them that our guests aren't really 'dining at The Wellington', they are having dinner with Rebecca! We educate them about the product through sampling (why rib eye is better than fillet, how our artisan chips are made, what wine is best with which dish etc.) and encourage them to get closer, to warmly interact with customers – owning the experience. I can unequivo-cally say that our order takers really buy into what we are doing: they are passionate about our product and know why it is good for the customer (both in terms of quality and value). This creates great customer relationships!

Alex Marsh, Commercial Director, Loungers
On Line and Co-Worker Training Delivery

Pre-opening training is handled by different GMs who are outstanding in various areas: compliance/safety, floor service and cocktail/coffee training, for instance... with food production being taught by two chefs: one who has a real talent for administration/preparation and another who is a superb cook... all are enthusiastic and passionate about their areas of expertise... My philosophy is that keeping things local is best... best practice training and the swapping of people/resources is best done locally rather than centrally... One of the main by-products of this is that managers and staff from different sites in my Area create *close* bonds between one another... This is what creates a real team at portfolio level... people like helping others because it makes them feel good – it raises their sense of self-esteem... It also keeps them close to the customer and local community... GMs/head chefs from one site, having covered for, trained and worked in other sites get to know their staff and customers... This gives them insight into other businesses but also creates trust, **confidence**, understanding and mutual respect... The people in this business are taught to be mobile, agile and flexible... It is not just about *their* site or *their* people: it is about the wider Area and business... the contribution they can make... [*Do you incentivise people for this behaviour?*] Not through cash – you don't need to... For these behaviours (which I demonstrate myself) we celebrate through giving out ad hoc gifts (premium knives to head chefs, for example), going for fun days out and covering units to let all the staff have a fun night out... We are one team in this Area... every job is as important as the other... helping one another out makes us all stronger, happier!

Reg Sindall, ex-EVP Group Resources, Burberry
On Alignment of Training with Service Ethos

With regards to service training, simplicity and consistency of approach [i.e. *values alignment*] are the most important factors... The service delivery system at Burberry was called the *'Burberry Experience'* which all employees were made conversant with, whatever their level, position, function or location... interestingly this programme... which was easily understandable and digestible... had been developed through empirical analysis of the [values and] behaviours of the best sales associates globally and then packaged as a consistent approach to drive *intentional, passionate, purposeful* and *confident* behaviours...

Equip Skills (generating CONFIDENCE) – Six Key Points

- Simple core objective (e.g. 'you are ladies and gentlemen serving ladies and gentlemen')
- Technical skills for quality and consistency of delivery
- Behavioural skills for emotional connection with guests
- Cognitive skills for operational problem solving
- Line manager and co-worker training delivery
- Meaningful accreditation and rewards for training certification

5. ENERGISE SERVICE – Lead (Generating ENTHUSIASM)

The fifth moment of truth is energising service providers through *direct* on-the-job leadership and management practices. Many of the emotional moments of truth we outline in this book touch upon the organisational climate in which service providers operate and the positive interventions that require application by senior leaders to provide the right context within which staff can operate effectively. This section deals with 'where the rubber hits the road', namely: the individual *shift battles* where operators interact directly with their customers. It is this moment of truth – where a multiple customer 'touches' are applied by service providers – which will determine the success or failure of the enterprise. The question at this moment is how well-equipped are *frontline leaders* to inspire, motivate and instruct their charges in the pursuance of outstanding, memorable and uplifting service? The answer, alas, for many organisations is poorly or not at all! Having thrown bodies onto the frontline and over-promoted the 'last men standing' that have hung around (presumably because they are unable to get jobs elsewhere), many service organisations have a line leadership capability that is inadequately prepared to cope with the challenges they face in the trading sessions they are confronted with. Here line management is more intent on 'surviving' with an *apathetic* and disillusioned skeleton staff, rather than 'raising the bar' on successive shifts.

Why is this so? Obviously several explanations relate back to what we have written about before: inattention to quality hiring, induction and training practices. But it also can be explained by a lack of understanding amongst senior managers – brought about through excessive distance and detachment from 'the front' – as to what qualities and actions are required to lead in the heat of the shift battle. For that is how we would describe it – a battle! This is a theatre of war in which aligned, motivated and well-resourced personnel vigorously achieve clear pre-defined goals. Great service companies understand this. Their senior people regularly go back to the floor to experience frontline reality and, consequently, are able to form a strong view on what exemplary shift leadership looks and feels like. They understand that at its heart lies the need for shift leaders to generate *enthusiasm* and passion for the task at hand – a verve, zeal and fervour to delight customers. But how is this shaped and achieved? Our belief is that the main factors underlying line leadership that enthuses service providers include: good planning and organisation, energetic modelling of required behaviours, adaptive 'situational' styles of leadership, the ability to take rapid decisions and protect people's backs when the going gets tough.

- **Set up for success** – the first thing that effective line managers do – something that is an *absolutely essential prerequisite* to successful trading sessions – is set up for success. What do we mean by this? Way before the shift battle commences, line managers plan and organise what will be required, based on their intelligence about what the customer requirements will be in any given session. Taking into account all available factors (timeslot, day-part, seasonality, promotional drives etc.), what resources does (s)he need to deploy, in which sections, at what time to achieve optimal outcomes. What objectives and goals do personnel require in order to, first, achieve the organisation's expectations and, second, engender a *feeling of accomplishment* and delight when they have been achieved? In short, they define what success looks like and put the resources in place to ensure it happens! The skill here lies in ensuring that all the 'moving parts' of the operation knit together effectively.

  So, successful hospitality line managers, for instance, will not concentrate on front-of-house at the exclusion back-of-house operations (including essential details such as clean, comfortable and functional staff rest rooms). In order to ensure a seamless, harmonious service session they will take a holistic view of their planning, including contributions and viewpoints from all of their section heads and business-critical personnel. They will then make sure that these plans are briefed out effectively (either in sessional huddles or in daily 'order of the day' notes). The point we are making is this: very often business books stress leadership philosophies such as 'servant leadership' and/or 'values-based leadership' as being the lodestones of business excellence, but we would argue that a good dose of basic *managerial practice* (i.e. *capacity to plan, organise, communicate and measure*) is required to ensure the fundamental elements are in place for success. In SAS parlance – to extend the military metaphor – "perfect planning prevents piss poor performance".

- **Energetic modelling** – the second thing effective line managers do in order to execute the plan is energise staff by personally modelling the required behaviours. In a previous research exercise examining leadership behaviour, we captured a case study from a retail operations manager from Sainsbury's, one of the UK's most successful supermarket chains, who reflected upon changing a general manager in one of his stores *precisely* because of the poor behaviours he modelled on the floor:

…when I took over the patch a year and a half ago, I knew that one of my stores (which accounts for 10% of the overall sales in my area) would be undergoing a multi-million-pound investment, increasing its size by nearly 30% to increase the general merchandise and clothing area. The store manager that was in place had been appointed by my predecessor, having followed in an extremely popular GM. This GM, unlike the one he followed in, *lacked buy-in and followership in the store. Colleagues complained that he was rarely seen on the floor and seemed to hide away in his office – staff pick up on messages from the GM pretty quickly: if the GM is in a bad mood or is invisible, morale throughout the store can change quite dramatically! Consequently, standards were* not where I wanted them to be, units were uncared for and random rubbish seemed scattered about every time I came in. The mystery customer and availability scores of this store were not where I wanted them to be.

So what I did was bring his personal development review forwards and was completely honest with him: "this is how the previous ROM viewed you, but I think you are in the underachieving box". I also followed up with lots of one-to-ones and 'visits with a purpose' to put him on the right track. The upshot was that he decided to leave the company and work for one of our competitors. This enabled me to *appoint a GM from a store nearby who is a great leader* to oversee the 36-week refurbishment cycle. He managed it with great success: sales disruption figures were managed to target and excellent mystery customer (+8%) and availability (+1.5%) scores were maintained throughout. *The new GM fits the culture of the store, is visible, has great leadership skills and colleague satisfaction is very high*! I dread to think what might have happened if the previous GM had handled this project!

Great line mangers in service businesses set the dynamic tone through their deportment, disposition and aura. They are psychologically close to the action rather than distant: interested rather than detached, inquisitive rather than ignorant, energetic rather than apathetic. It is not just their words that create a positive vibe: it is their presence and body language which fizz and crackle with energy, modelling the required behaviours and enthusing others to imitate them.

- **Situational style fit** – whilst emphasising the importance of positive behavioural modelling, it is important to recognise that at certain times and in certain situations, managers will have to adopt different styles in order to get things done. In times of crisis or in circumstances requiring courageous leadership, managers will have to adopt a task-driven approach in order to drive things through – particularly when some of their people are (in Hersey and Blanchard's terms) "unable, unwilling or insecure". A more delegative style is appropriate in situations where staff feel "able, willing and confident" but still, the line manager must have an eye out for changes in personal and trading circumstances that might force them to take a firmer hand. The point is this: whilst line managers should consistently exude a positive 'can do' attitude, they should be capable of intuitively adapting their style of one-to-one and team management to the situations and scenarios they are confronted with. One can still be positive whilst being firm and directional: positivity is not only related to delegative and involving styles of management! Of course, if people are unable to transition out of *don't know or don't care* states of mind, the line manager's only option is to get rid of them as soon as is practically possible to maintain the morale and momentum of their team. Such actions, in themselves, will result in unbelievable energy dividends from the remaining team members, who will feel liberated from having to carry free riding, energy-sapping passengers.

- **Rapid decision making** – in the heat of the shift battle, staff that are desperately engaged in satisfying customer demands either require the autonomy to make instant decisions (this will be dealt with in a subsequent section) or – where they have to refer to a higher authority – the means to get rapid answers to maintain their credibility and momentum. In order to do this, line managers require a high degree of courage. Why? Because often, many issues are not covered by the 'rule book' and they certainly can't take their operational manuals out onto the floor. They will have to make judgement calls – compensating customers for lapses in product quality, for instance – that sit outside prescribed policies and procedures. They must also be prepared to stand behind their decisions if they go wrong. Either way, calling it right or wrong, line managers will gain respect from their people if they are prepared to take decisions, easing the burden and lightening the load of responsibility that their people feel at times. Again, this means that line managers must be 'in the business' and, at the very least, have an open-door policy so that staff feel that they can approach them at any time to resolve pressing issues.

- **Get people's backs** – but the one factor that will really generate followership and teamship for the line manager is a willingness to stand behind staff in difficult circumstances. We recently asked the CEO of a major casual dining brand in the UK – during the course of our investigation into high-performance brand leadership – what the single most important thing he did for his people was and he said:

…during the course of service we are (increasingly) getting highly emotional complaints that filter through to me either though comment cards or social media… comments like "my meal was delayed by five minutes and you've destroyed my life!"… In this age of instant gratification, people want it perfect, they want it now and they won't tolerate any genuine mistakes… my job is to differentiate between genuine complaints and emotive outpourings… Very often I've stood up on their behalf to hideously biased criticism, which is often expressed in quite rude terms… swearing, bad language, personal attacks… I won't stand for this… this means that my people know that I've got their backs… and I know they respect me for it…

As we have discussed elsewhere in this book, customer expectations – amongst all segments of the market – are increasing at a rapid rate, with reactions to perceptions that they have been 'let down' becoming more public and aggressive. This means that line managers must discriminate between merited criticism and venal outpourings to establish the true facts and, where their staff have been the victims of unjustified attacks, back them up accordingly.

So, in addition to all the other moments of truth in this book – critical employment cycle stages where great service companies aim to generate positive feelings amongst their people – organisations must pay attention to how service providers are energised by face-to-face, direct line-management practices. So for obvious reasons, many organisations concentrate on giving line managers 'hard' technical skills to expedite their responsibilities, neglecting to bolster their 'softer' leadership skills which they require to energise and *enthuse* their people. Perhaps they assume these behavioural skills will already be there or – more likely – they are unwilling to invest time and money in training that (in their eyes) offers little tangible payback. This is highly mistaken. Teaching line managers how to manage and lead before, during and after the heat of the shift battle will pay dividends not only in terms of staff morale but also in the sustainability of the business. The organisation will be able to absorb shocks and react accordingly due to the fact that it has a highly resilient, well-led frontline. Giving line managers a solid grounding and insight into how to organise resources, model positive behaviours, adapt their styles appropriately to different situations, make rapid decisions and stand behind their people is a worthwhile investment. This is particularly true when it is coupled with recognition and incentive systems that reward and reinforce the right behaviours – something that will be addressed in the next section.

CASE STUDY 12 – **LEADER REFLECTIONS ON LEADING THE LINE (JACK & ALICE AND JENS HOFMA)**

Vanessa Hall, Co-Founder, Jack & Alice
On How Inspirational Leaders 'Orchestrate the Shift'

What do great shift leaders do? I like to look upon them as *conductors of the shift orchestra who*:

- **Model the tone** – great shift leaders in hospitality treat every guest as if they were a guest in their own home. They engage with guests on the floor by assisting staff – welcoming, serving, checking back – in short modelling great hospitality behaviours...

- **Simplify operations** – they also set things up for success by keeping things simple. Both before and during the shift, they get staff to concentrate on the two or three things in their role that they should concentrate upon to give the guest an outstanding experience...

- **Pick up the edge** – finally, in my view, they take away the anxiety from their team by sorting out issues and resolving problems (be these IT, difficult customers, late orders etc.). This takes the stress away from staff so that they can enjoy their shift and operate naturally and enthusiastically – returning again for their next one! Yes, great shift leaders not only model great hospitality and define (with great clarity to what people should be doing) – they are also extremely effective at spotting and resolving wobbles in the heat of the shift battle!

Jens Hofma, CEO Pizza Hut
On Modelling Leadership Behaviour

One thing I did that reinforced what I wanted the organisation to do was to personally go back to the floor... Many senior people think they can keep in touch with what is happening on the ground through 'dog and pony show' visits... I didn't want our solutions for the brand to be over-theoretical or conceptual... I needed to get up close with the customer and our teams through working a shift a week... At first, I didn't tell anybody for three or four months: it was important for it not to be seen as stage managed... It gave me an excellent insight into what worked and the psychology of our team... Really *my behaviour was 'inverting the pyramid'* – I was closing down distance by working at the point of impact... I still do a shift a month now – I think it not only helps me understand the business better but also *signals the central importance of our customers and restaurant teams to the wider organisation...*

6. EXCITE BEHAVIOURS – Recognise (Generating JOY)

The sixth moment of truth in our cycle of key employment practices is exciting staff through reward, recognition and praise: making people feel *joyful* about the fact that their contributions are highly valued, rather than feeling ***exasperated*** that their efforts are being overlooked or taken for granted! Research – such as that done by Gallup – consistently highlights the fact that people who feel they are rewarded equitably and receive regular recognition and praise are more productive, have better relationships with their colleagues, have higher levels of satisfaction, better safety records, lower blood pressure and are more likely to stay. Indeed, one of the major reasons that is cited by people who quit their jobs is that they do not feel appreciated. Organisations that fail to have vibrant formal or informal reward and recognition mechanisms are soulless receptacles of drudgery, often characterised by high levels of turnover, low levels of engagement and inconsistent levels of quality. This inevitably begs the question: why would any organisation set itself up to fail in such a manner? Again, short-termist, output-obsessed, transactional leadership is to blame: leaders who focus on results rather than people, knowing the cost of everything but the value of nothing.

Great service organisations are the complete opposite. They recognise that fair, transparent and motivational reward and recognition systems lie at the heart of every successful organisation. They set themselves up for success by investing in reward and recognition systems that *satisfy*, *surprise* and *delight* their people. That is not to say they squander resources in over-inflated salaries and untargeted, unmerited incentive programmes – quite the opposite. They think hard about the behaviours they wish to stimulate and the reward and recognition mechanisms that will fit. Also, this is an exercise that is not merely outsourced to the HR Department, but a process which is very much driven and led by senior leaders within the organisation who are highly conscious of both its symbolic and practical benefits to their company. To this extent, reward and recognition systems that excite and motivate are – we believe – characterised by five main features: they incentivise service behaviours, specifically reward skills and competencies acquisition, give key players 'skin in the game', enable teams to celebrate success together and permit planned spontaneity, so that managers can 'catch people doing it right'.

- **Incentivise service behaviours** – we have already made the point that excellent service companies have equitable and transparent reward systems where – in relative terms at the very least – individuals feel that they are remunerated fairly for the work they do. That is to say, when they look at how 'similar work for similar value' jobs are rewarded elsewhere, they feel comfortable that they are not being disadvantaged or ripped off. Also, when they examine pay differentials within the organisation they work at, they feel that there isn't a disproportionate gap between what they earn and what their bosses take home. In the UK the John Lewis Partnership is often cited as an exemplar organisation in this regard: the take-home pay of the senior leadership team is a modest multiple of an average shop assistant's wage, bolstering feelings of fairness and equanimity.

But how should incentives be applied to reinforce and animate the correct behaviours? The first things to say is: what gets measured, gets managed but what gets rewarded, gets done! With regards to service organisations, incentives that are targeted at rewarding staff for excellent customer service are more likely to result in the provision of an outstanding customer experience. Sector-leading hospitality organisations, for instance, will tie a proportion of their team incentives to customer satisfaction score ratings and ensure that – where tipping for service occurs – the 'tronque' (i.e. tips pool) is spread out evenly throughout the front-of-house and back-of-house teams to preserve and enhance a one-team mentality. They certainly don't misappropriate or abuse the tipping system – as some urban casual dining companies were found to be doing recently – by raiding it to get rates of pay over the minimum wage threshold! Secondly, service-led incentives that work are (in Peter Ducker's parlance) SMART – meaning specific, measurable, achievable, realistic and time-related. Sometimes, service incentives are linked to measures that can be manipulated or massaged: for instance, NPS returns or TripAdvisor comments that are filled in by friends or colleagues to boost perceptions of service performance! Third, progress against target is communicated regularly, potential payouts from the scheme are frequent (to sustain levels of focus and motivation) and payment is made immediately, rather than held back for irritating, complex 'qualifying' or 'hurdle rate' reasons.

- **Reward skills and competencies** – in addition to incentivising service, great service companies frequently link pay rises and increments to skills and knowledge acquisition. Why do they do this? First, to encourage staff to value learning. Second, to build a solid platform of capability within their organisation. Third – and most importantly – to give their people a sense of aspiration and achievement. In the UK, sector-leading organisations such as McDonald's have found that linking pay to skills certification has not only improved retention and morale, but also widened the pool from which they are able to promote talent. Their 'stars' system enables team members to move through several training-related pay increments, onto first-line supervisory levels and beyond. Tellingly, over 50 per cent of their senior management in the UK in 2015 originated from team-member level, having progressed through ranks by achieving mandatory accreditations that were certified and rewarded under the auspices of their 'stars' programme. At a national level too, in the UK, the revival of the apprenticeship system (that grants incentives and tax breaks to participant organisations) has further fuelled the notion that connecting pay and progression with certified skills acquisition is of positive benefit both to companies and 'entry-level' employees.

- **'Skin in the game'** – promoting a sense of equity around rates of pay, incentivising service behaviours and rewarding skills attainment will ensure that organisations have a happier, more productive 'ship'. Levels of commitment, however, will also be boosted if, in addition to these mechanisms, staff and managers have an actual share in the ownership of the business, giving them a deep-rooted, vested interest in its success. In the past, the UK government has encouraged staff ownership in publically quoted companies by offering tax concessions on employee share-ownership schemes, enabling organisations to offer generously discounted and/or free shares to employees. Smaller unlisted or privately owned concerns have sometimes set up shadow schemes that grant employees redeemable 'shadow shares' that vest at pre-set times. Of course, the strength of loyalty and commitment such employee-focused schemes generate can be questionable – particularly if the firm is trading badly or the amounts of shares on offer are inconsequentially low. Where 'skin in the game' programmes work particularly well, however, is usually at store management or franchisee–owner level where pivotal players are granted a piece of the action. For instance, in the UK casual dining operators like Nando's – particularly in its early incarnation – and pub restaurant companies like the Peach Pub Company have operated schemes which have granted their site managers actual or notional shares of the company that are linked to variables such as length of service, site performance and growth of the organisation. Such schemes can be extremely powerful – spreading the gains of the organisation to the places in the company where it matters most: amongst those closest to the service teams and their customers!

- **Celebrate success together** – alongside these formal, individualistic mechanisms of reward and recognition, collective occasions that bring the 'tribe' together to celebrate successes and achievements also serve to energise and excite. Such events represent a public opportunity to showcase, recognise and reward the behaviours that organisations are seeking to propagate, namely: outstanding service, fantastic standards, great ideas, exceptional levels of discretionary effort and exemplary team work. These celebrations can take place in small daily gatherings (buzz or shift meetings) or at larger set-piece events that create powerful, enduring memories, such as the events that Chris Moore organised during his tenure as CEO of Domino's:

> …at DPG, in addition to district and regional meetings, we held two major set-piece events which were *deliberately inclusive…* In October every year we had a managers' conference where we 'got them pumped up' for Xmas… Our key event was the DPG awards

ceremony in March/April where, after having business and information sessions at the beginning, we had a big bash at the end... But the point is this: we didn't only invite franchisees, we also invited their partners (who bear as much, if not more of the burden!) and franchisees invited managers, along with other staff members and drivers that had been nominated for the top awards... the mood and spirit were phenomenal – it really glued us together for the year... even some of the franchisees and leadership team joined me in getting dressed up on stage (I made a great Marilyn Monroe and a cracking Queen!) and we made fun of ourselves... **We chanted** *"Who Are We? Domino's! What Are We? Number One! What Do We Do? Sell More Pizzas, Have More Fun!"*... This 'anglicised Americanism', as I call it, might seem trite to cynics, but it worked: for a few days we were altogether... bonding... celebrating winning... with precious little sense of hierarchy and looking forward to winning together over the next year.

Clearly, such large-scale productions – exciting, dramatic and theatrical as they are – not only serve reward and recognition purposes but also as a bonding opportunity, to rally the organisation around a coherent identity that fosters a tangible sense of buy-in, pride and belief. It is also a forum where people from disparate parts of the organisation can learn to value one another's contributions and share tacit knowledge in an unthreatening, relaxed setting. The enduring symbols of these celebratory occasions – photos and videos that can be uploaded onto social media – ensure that such moments are captured forever, giving participants evocative artefacts that they can publically show their colleagues, family and friends and reflect upon fondly, long after the event.

- **Planned spontaneity and catching people doing it right** – all of the recognition mechanisms we've described so far are fairly well signposted and planned, but one of the most powerful means of recognising people involves the element of surprise. We call this 'planned spontaneity' – occasions when managers recognise people 'on the spot' with heartfelt praise and (possibly) reward. We have seen this working best in situations where managers make it their mission to 'catch people doing it right'. The opening case study in this book captured the moment when Tony saw this in action:

...Fred said "come on, *lets catch somebody doing something right!*" So we go through the kitchen and walk past a nice Mexican chap who's making guacamole with the menu out, the recipe book out and all the correct ingredients, well turned out in a pristine uniform. So Fred calls an all-store meeting. All the staff gather together and Fred starts to explain: "I'd like to take this opportunity... because I've seen something today that I regret and feel guilty about. We have an employee that works in our kitchen that has come in here for the last six years every day making the most fabulous guacamole. Even though he knows exactly how to do it he's always got his recipe book open, he's got everything measured, he's got quality ingredients which he's inspected and you know what – you have the pleasure to serve fabulous guacamole and the guests have the honour to eat it! This guy is a backbone of this organisation and we are guilty of taking him for granted – we need to say THANK YOU!" Of course, everyone knew who Fred was talking about and were so moved that tears had started flooding down people's faces and this poor chap was beside himself... then Fred said: "Hosea, we all want you to know how much we appreciate you and the quality of your work. Consistent high performance is often taken for granted and the spectacular one offs acclaimed by the crowd, but to the team, the true heroes are hidden heroes who go about their work in a consistent, dependable and predictable manner, unselfishly working for the benefit of others. These are truly our most valuable players..." Fred then produced an MVP (Most Valuable Person) medal and pinned it onto Hosea's chest in military fashion, shook his hand and hugged him to huge applause and cheering from all the restaurant staff...

This story is emotionally charged: a spontaneous act of heart-warming recognition that moves people to shed tears of joy. Why? Firstly, because the recipient is deserving of the accolade. He is widely acknowledged amongst his peers as being exactly as Fred describes him - a 'hidden hero', somebody who uncomplainingly and professionally goes about his daily routine, producing great guacamole that the store can be rightfully proud of. Second, Fred's act of spontaneous generosity, which enlivens a day of humdrum normality, shows that the company cares about somebody's contribution, when usually it would be ignored or taken for granted. Third, what Fred has done is the diametric opposite of what many managers do, namely: fulfilling an audit and checking role to catch people out in order to correct behaviour. Fred, on the other hand, catches people doing it right in order to powerfully reinforce and reward correct behaviour.

In summary, organisations need to animate the right behaviours amongst their people through purposeful and exciting reward and recognition mechanisms. As the final section of this book highlights, recognition and praise release the brain chemical dopamine, a neurotransmitter that causes feelings of pleasure and *joy*. Having received the hit as a reward for certain behaviours, humans will seek 'chemical repetition' by repeating the same behaviours. Scientists have estimated that a 5:1 praise-to-criticism ratio optimises human dopamine releases. That is to say, managers should praise their charges five times more than criticise them in order to shape positive behaviours. In addition, recognition will also have a high impact when individuals are nominated by their peers or customers rather than just by their managers. Peer recognition is a profound appreciation by those who know, more than anybody else, the discretionary effort that has been expended away from the limelight. In organisations where people's efforts go unappreciated in (sometimes) compliant and exploitative environments, emotional bank accounts will run dry pretty quickly with disastrous knock-on effects upon quality and service. Organisations that actively incentivise service behaviours, reward skills and competencies progression, give key field operators 'skin in the game', ensure that their people celebrate success together and spontaneously 'catch people doing it right' are more likely – in addition to the interventions we highlight elsewhere in this book – to excite and motivate their teams. Particularly when they want them to act responsibly, autonomously and with flexibility to satisfy customer demands, as the next section will discuss.

CASE STUDY 13 – **LEADER REFLECTIONS ON RECOGNITION THAT EXCITES (INNVENTURE, LOUNGERS, BURBERRY AND GENERAL MANAGER VOICES)**

Chris Gerrard, Founder, Innventure
On Incentivising Service

Crucially, order takers keep their tips and tip in to their service providers. This serves as an instant reward for their *discretionary effort and their levels of customer engagement*. It also means that these roles are highly prized within the units: staff starting off behind the bar, or as runners, aspire to these positions. Also, order takers – if they are really successful – will always be motivated to work on key peak shifts, meaning that our 'A Team' is always matched to the busiest sessions. Order taking in our businesses is seen as a prized privilege!

**Paul Daynes, GHRD St Gobain, ex-HRD Musgraves
(Budgens and Londis)**
On Skin in the Game

Musgrave was a family-owned franchised food retail business that had successfully built supermarket (Supervalu) and convenience (Centra) franchised concepts within their core Irish market. Gaining either of these franchises in Ireland was looked upon as being highly valuable – Musgraves deployed extremely generous terms... they imposed no caps on how much franchisees could earn – believing that tying franchisees in *through chains of gold* was mutually beneficial to both parties... Musgrave had an astonishingly frank and benevolent core value of *'don't be greedy'*... as a family-run business they believed in long-term sustainable relationships with their franchisees based on mutual respect founded upon a fair division of the spoils... as I said, Musgrave was quite keen to lock its franchisees in with 'chains of gold' so that they didn't move to other symbol franchised groups and – because of the high value of the franchise – operated the franchise to unbelievably high standards (a must, given the 'fresh quality' ethos of the brand)... I still know several of the original 'corporate franchisees' today who are still there, have done extremely well out of the arrangement and are (still) unbelievably committed to the franchisor and the brand!

Alex Marsh (Commercial Director, Loungers) and Reg Sindall (ex-EVP, Burberry)
On Celebrating Success

Alex Marsh: [Do you incentivise people for this behaviour?] Not through cash – you don't need to... For these behaviours (which I demonstrate myself) we *celebrate* through giving out ad hoc gifts (premium knives to head chefs, for example), going for fun days out and covering units to let all the staff have a fun night out... We are one team on this Area... every job is important as the other... helping one another out makes us all *feel stronger, happier!*...

Reg Sindall: underpinned by constant endorsement through senior management making frequent international store visits, regular regional conferences and awards ceremonies, where store, call-centre and HQ-level service excellence (i.e. politeness, knowledge and quality) was publically recognised and rewarded – *spreading joy!*... such events also provided excellent networking opportunities across our international operations...

General Manager Voices from the MSc Multi-Unit Leadership and Strategy Programme –
On Spontaneous Recognition

- **Personal Touch** – "What I like about my present boss is that he remembers the names and interests of my people... In fact, he spends a good deal of his time talking to my staff about their families and sport... It's the *personal touch* – showing an interest – being human!... You get a lot back [in effort] from that..." (GM, Food Service)

  "My manager is good at remembering our birthdays and always delivers a present... a few bottles of wine or a tin of sweets at Xmas. It's a personal touch and we really appreciate it... Actually, *we would walk over hot coals for him!*" (GM, Leisure)

- **Praise** – "Unlike some of the managers I've had before, this one doesn't send out sinister district emails praising a few and then dumping on the rest by *highlighting people at the bottom of league tables in red*... actually what he does is recognises how far some people have come on certain measures and *praises* improvement as well as top performance..." (GM, Retail)

- **Recognition** – "My gaffer is very good at *recognising effort...* picking the phone up to me and saying 'well done', particularly on Mondays after busy sessions over the weekend to give me a bit of a lift or after we've done something particularly good... like great sales, mystery customer or safety visits... unlike other managers I've had, I don't hear his voice and think 'here's another bollocking!'" (GM, Hospitality)

Excite Behaviours (generating JOY) – Six Key Points

- Incentivise great service behaviours
- Reward skills acquisition ('££s for skills')
- Give up some 'skin in the game'
- Celebrate with the tribe
- 'Catch', recognise and reward people doing it right
- Praise five times more than you correct

---

7. EMPOWER ACTIONS – Autonomy (Generating TRUST)

The seventh emotional moment of truth in our cycle of employment is empowering frontline staff to do everything they can to delight the customer. Why is this important? First, it is a mistake to regard service businesses as homogenous: units serve micro-markets and demographics from facilities that will have small – but nuanced – differences. Service providers need a degree of flexibility to accommodate these divergences. Second, in today's markets – partly driven by digital experiences – customers have an increasing preference for customisation and individualisation. A 'one size fits all' principal can no longer be applied to products and services: those doing the serving must therefore be granted some discretion to modify the product to the customer's needs and preferences. Third – as Daniel Pink argued in his masterful treatise on leadership – younger workers today hanker after some degree of autonomy that allows them to both feel in control and express their own personality.

But what do empowering organisations look like and what barriers prevent them from flourishing? Generally, empowerment is bolstered by a number of factors, including: company policies that define it, embedding the correct skills and competencies which allow it to flourish successfully and strong leadership modelling at the apex of the organisation which constantly reinforces it as a 'good thing'. Typical barriers include: recruiting inappropriate people for roles, not granting them proper resources to do the job, insufficient training to give them confidence and service providers losing heart because the complaints they deal with on a daily basis remain unresolved. In addition, companies that schizophrenically swing from 'loose to tight' – granting autonomy at one moment and then moving swiftly to compliance the next – are likely to spread *frustration*, confusion, fear and mistrust amongst their staff, disabling the chances of an empowerment culture ever taking hold. But as we say, the case for empowering frontline staff in the current business environment has never been stronger. So – accepting some of the best practice features we have already mentioned – how should companies aspire to set up an empowerment culture that breeds *trust* and confidence amongst their employees? We recommend five main factors: specifying flexibility within a fixed frame, permitting signature acts of self-expression, encouraging continuous process improvement to occur, sanctioning employees to apply patch ups and workarounds to policies that don't work and allowing what we call 'added value deviance' to take place without major retribution.

- **Flexibility within a fixed frame** – whilst empowering organisations centrally mandate various fixed policies, procedures and practices, they generally allow some flexibility for local autonomous behaviour. Some build clear '*no go*', '*check then go*' and '*go*' rules into their operational model. They do this for two aforementioned reasons: first, to build a degree of local responsiveness and agility into their business model at micro-market level; and second, to enrich frontline operators' job roles through providing a certain degree of autonomy and self-expression. Paradoxically organisations that claim to allow a certain degree of local autonomy – such as IKEA – actually find that they are able to extract better 'core' control of their operations in exchange! The degree to which operators will be granted 'flexibility within a frame' will be dependent on two principal factors: the culture of the organisation (a belief in 'tight' compliance or 'loose' empowerment) and/or the degree of 'hard' tightly prescribed or 'soft' customised branding. The *fixed* element of operations incorporates centrally mandated policies usually incorporating the brand blueprint and standard operating procedures (BOH and FOH). These elements underpin the efficiency of the organisation – ensuring consistency and dependability of execution – and are regularly monitored/audited to ensure conformance and compliance. *Flexible* elements offer prescribed ways of working that might allow service operators a certain amount of latitude with regards to addressing the local market (e.g. service 'touches, recovery and rectification', local range, promotions and social media 'marketing' etc.). However, interestingly, some organisations have gone further than prescribing a catch-all model, segmenting their businesses according to capability and performance. Pizza Hut UK, for instance, has four 'autonomy classifications' for its estate, where units are allowed to exercise local discretion, contingent upon the financial performance and experience of the operators. In short, high-performing units with experienced managers (Grade 1 Units) are given far more 'denominated freedoms' than those that are underperforming and/or have inexperienced/underperforming managers (Grade 4 Units). Others, like Federal Express, deploy different empowerment standards at different levels, especially with regard to customer refunds, where phone representatives require no prior approval up to $250, with supervisors having an upper limit of $10,000.

- **Signature acts of self-expression** – in addition to prescribed flexibility, some companies actively encourage staff to express their personality by allowing them to include a 'signature act of self-expression'. What is this? TGI Friday's, for instance, has a very tight customer service cycle which it expects its 'teamers' to follow: it ensures consistency and quality of operations. But within this cycle, teamers are permitted to include one 'heart-warming action' that allows them to personally connect with guests (singing, doing card tricks, dancing etc.). It is not that the company is trying to turn them into performing monkeys: rather, it is recognising the fact that their staff have extrovert personalities. Allowing them to express themselves in a fun way, gives them (and their guests!) a high degree of enjoyment and satisfaction.

- **Improvement contributions** – being empowered to respond to customer needs is critical, but staff also need to feel that they are empowered to change things within their organisation. In the Introduction, we referred to Mathew Syed's book *Black Box*

Thinking in which he argued that organisations that actively encouraged a culture of 'problem disclosure' and then took steps to remedy them had lower quality malfunctions than those that didn't. This most certainly applies in service organisations. High trust environments will prevail where staff feel that the people 'in the clouds' are listening to their suggestions for improvement. How should companies go about this? Earlier in the book we talked about how senior leaders should get 'into' rather than sit 'on' the business, watching, listening, processing and swiftly acting upon defects and/or opportunities. Some organisations, however, have gone about this more formally and rigorously. Inditex, owner of Zara, makes daily contact with stores around the world, from its base in Spain, to understand how customers and managers feel about its products and processes. Sainsbury's has a daily 'operations call' between a senior director (who can get things done) and a representative from each of its districts, to act immediately upon practical suggestions to improve operations. Others have successfully embedded a 'total quality' approach, where TQM systems have been set up to systematically resolve issues and problems at the coalface. Whatever the mechanism, however, the main point is this. Empowering cultures do not only give employees the necessary wherewithal to deal with customer needs and requests: they also listen to the *feedback* staff give as to how things can be improved internally in order to function more effectively and profitably. Those that don't – or merely pay lip service to it – run the risk of having an organisation populated by malcontents who feel powerless to change anything, however egregiously offensive some of the things they're being asked to do are to the laws of common sense!

- **Patch ups and workarounds** – in some instances, however, managers in service business will feel that they need to take matters into their own hands to make improvements: actions which we label 'patch ups and workarounds'. Often, given the distance of the centre from the rest of the business, its failure to use (or listen to) operator expertise in the conception of new change initiatives, coupled with its lack of insight into the minutiae of unit operations (due to few operators transitioning into jobs in the centre), many change initiatives might be ill-conceived or badly thought out. The service operator now has a choice: does (s)he accept the change initiative lock, stock and barrel or seek to make (legal) alterations that make the initiatives more workable? For sure, many operators, fearing sanctions from the centre for non-compliance, will adopt the former route, passively accepting what they have been told to do. Braver, more self-confident ones (a state usually borne through experience) will, however, not accept the status quo, either suggesting modifications to the centre immediately to enhance chances of the initiative's success or make adaptations themselves following consultation with their teams. In the first instance, operators will make modifications by *patching up* the deficiencies of the change initiative. This means that, having understood the detail of the change initiative and consulted with their colleagues or team, (s)he will make improvements that will add value to the efficiency and effectiveness of the initiative. In exceptional circumstances, operators will *work around* certain initiatives because of their poor conception/design. This is not to say that they fully reject the objectives underpinning the initiative: workarounds fulfil the main intentions or *ends* of the initiative without any resort to the *means* suggested by the policy designers. This is a highly dangerous strategy that, in the hands of inexperienced or over-exited operators, can foster and embed bad behaviour. Living solely by the dictum that the ends justify the means can lead to chaos and anarchy in service businesses. Nonetheless, there are instances where, after mature and rational consideration, implementing a workaround strategy can pay dividends!

- **Added value deviance (AVD)** – on very few occasions, successful (maverick!) operators will breach company standards, rules and procedures if they believe either that the law is an ass or that there are better ways of doing things. This behaviour can be termed 'added value deviance' because whilst such behaviour might be deemed illegal by the organisation, it might actually serve to improve overall business performance. As stated, operators on the ground might be well ahead of technocrats at the centre in terms of what the customer expects and what might give them competitive advantage within local micro-markets. It is important to state however that added value deviance will only flourish under two conditions. First, it is only operable or sustainable within circles of trust where operators feel that they are protected by higher authorities who will shield them against punishment. Second, a strict code of personal conduct must apply. Short-termist, self-interested blatant cheating will have harmful long-term side effects on the network. There are some instances when over-exuberant (or desperate) operators have instituted policies in their own interests that have 'blown up the machine'!

In summary, organisations have put a lot of time and energy into enticing, hiring, onboarding and training great people: it stands to reason then that they should have the faith and confidence to give them a reasonable degree of *discretion* to service their customers to the best of their abilities. Likewise, they should put in sufficient *feedback* mechanisms that capture their views on how systems, processes and practices can be improved to give their customers an outstanding experience. They can do this through applying a 'flexibility within a frame' approach, allowing signature acts of self-expression, setting up appropriate improvement mechanisms/forums and benignly permitting operators to apply (merited) patchups and workarounds and experiment, on occasions, through what we term 'added value deviance'. We would offer two further insights. Firstly, whilst service providers and operators should be empowered to delight the customers that the organisation wants, they should – concomitantly – be given the discretionary power to discourage the customers the company doesn't want. Within retail and hospitality, in particular, permitting staff to sensitively move on customers who are destroying the experience for others will safeguard the integrity of the product for the core users. Secondly, empowerment should not be used as an excuse for cost-cutting (i.e. culling staff numbers in order to place *all* accountability on an exposed frontline). We both remember a colleague who – when the 'empowerment' concept was at its zenith in the 1990s – slashed his organisational headcount, saying to his people: "it's ok, I am going to make this a more devolved, empowered organisation... less hierarchical... but you are only empowered *when I tell you*!" In short, a rhetoric of empowerment should not hide a reality of compliance, otherwise major *trust* issues will pervade the company. But a truly empowered culture is a marvellous sight to behold – a place where creativity, flexibility and high levels of discretionary effort flourish. As the next section will demonstrate, this is particularly so when it is backed up by personal and career growth programmes that fire up *aspiration*.

CASE STUDY 14 – LEADER REFLECTIONS ON EMPOWERMENT AND TRUST (CASUAL DINING GROUP, PRINCIPAL HOTELS, ARCHIE'S ASDA, CO-OP FOOD TURNAROUND AND VALUE RESTAURANTS)

James Spragg, Chief Operating Officer of the Casual Dining Group
On Freedom and Trust

I have found that empowerment works if you set out clearly what you want the outcomes from people's behaviours to be. So you have to set very clear expectations. But… don't be too prescriptive. Obviously you have to make sure that people understand that they have to operate safely and legally, but you have to treat your team in an adult fashion: the way you would expect to be treated yourself. In most businesses there are lots of 'central tools' that are aimed at generating compliance and 'efficiency'. But over-indexing on these systems and processes can erode levels of agility, flexibility discretionary effort on the ground. People need to buy into, understand and *want* to do things. They aren't robots or machines. You must allow a degree of autonomy and freedom in a broad framework of trust. One should not let a few bad apples let that trust fall away!

Sean Wheeler, Director of People, Principal Hotels (ex-Dorchester Collection and Malmaison)
On 'Authors' and 'Editors'

…what we try and encourage is a sense of 'freedom within a fixed frame'. But fundamentally what David (the COO) and I do is go around the business saying to people "we trust you – this is your business: do the right thing by our guests!" At the moment at Principal (where we are still refining many of our core systems and policies) we need '*authors*' more than '*editors*'. What do I mean by this? Authors who – in the absence of rigidly defined policies or 'scripts' – take intuitive decisions that are the right ones for our guests. Rather than editors who interpret manuals or seek to implement a prescribed set of guidelines. We encourage our authors to take decisions and – if they make mistakes – reassure them that there will be no ramifications. We give them the confidence that we trust them. If they are acting within the boundaries of the brand promise and values, they will be acting within the best interests of both the guests and the organisation. You can't take a cookie-cutter approach to empowerment: you have to establish the broad parameters and then trust your people to get on with it in a trusting, conciliatory manner… We seek consistency but we also grant flexibility…

Helen Webb, Director of HR, Co-op Food Retail (formerly holder of senior HR and executive roles at Sainsbury's, Morrison's, ASDA, Aviva and M&S)
On Empowerment and Trust

[On creating a climate of empowerment at ASDA:] What the leaders of the business – Archie Norman and Allan Leighton – talked about all the time was getting 'ordinary people to do extraordinary things'... to this end they were advocates of giving people 'freedom within a framework': being clear on the core things that they expected, but granting colleagues the space to act creatively and express themselves... For instance, the famous 'Tell Archie' scheme actively encouraged colleagues to suggest ideas to improve the business to Archie Norman: *all* would be investigated for their potential... Archie and Alan were also highly visible in the business listening and learning; processing how they could improve the business by listening to their people... It is amazing to look back and reflect that so many of the people they gave permission to experiment so early in their careers – *trusted* to get it wrong as well as *trusted* to get it right! – are now scattered around UK and international retail in senior positions! ... How did it make people feel within ASDA at the time? ... it made them feel as if they were part of something fabulous... a place where everyone and everybody's opinions mattered... people really believed that they could make a difference... We won the UK's Best Place to Work award a number of times – and one of our highest scores was always 'I feel I have the tools and freedom to do my job to the best of my ability'...

[On creating a climate of empowerment at Co-op Food Retail:] Having been part of a turnaround team over the past three years (that has experienced significant success), one of the essential ingredients has, *first*, been getting people to reconnect with what we stand for; so we've spent a lot of time working with everyone in small groups talking through our purpose – going right back to the community-based philanthropic philosophies of our founding pioneers in 1844... we've backed this up by giving stores the hours to go out and develop deeper roots within their communities... *Second*, we've empowered our front-line colleagues by enabling them to remedy customer problems and issues on the spot rather than (as they did before) referring customers to central complaints... By restoring this sense of purpose and granting a greater degree of autonomy, we have won back the *trust* of our people and engendered a feeling of *pride* in the organisation...

Susie Palmer, Area Manager, Value Restaurants
On Autonomy AND Trust

I understood the need for localised marketing to drive footfall and reach new guests. An innovative proposition raised was regarding marketing 'boosts' on business Facebook pages which – for a fraction of the national marketing cost – could drive significant local guest awareness of the daily offers available. In this case, for just £12, one of my general managers had added 4,000 additional followers to his business's Facebook page by tactically advertising existing offers! However, the marketing team felt that this fell outside social-media policy guidelines and that as such it should not be acted upon. In this circumstance, I backed the GM... the opportunity was too great to miss and was being used by our competitors locally: the risk in my view was greater to not take advantage of this opportunity. I put some process around this and ensured that I had one lead manager accountable for regularly checking the content of these pages, but otherwise acted on *trust*. My managers wanted to do the right things for the right reasons and I was happy to support them in this within a protected environment... I believe the consistency of my actions is the bedrock of generating trust and engaging my team. I work on the basis of *informed autonomy and trust*... However, if trust is broken I act swiftly and will hold the individual to account. The amount of trust provided is directly related to the capability of the manager thereby mitigating unforeseen service performance issues!

Empower Action (generating TRUST) – Five Key Points

- Clearly state: 'go, check, no go'
- Allow signature acts of self-expression
- Create feedback loops: listen and act
- Permit local patch ups and workarounds
- Give discretionary power to discourage guests you don't want

8. ENRICH CAREERS – Develop (Generating HOPE)

The eighth moment of emotional truth for organisations in the employment cycle is career progression and development that enriches lives, creating a feeling of ***hope and aspiration*** amongst employees at all levels. Moment of Truth 4, 'Equip Skills', described the technical, cognitive and behavioural skills programmes that were required to instil confidence – especially amongst newbies to the organisation – and these do provide a platform for career development. But in addition, we would argue that *transparent, integrated talent development mechanisms* which give staff *at all levels* within the organisation the opportunity to *grow and progress* are particularly important. Often these progression channels are indistinct and vague within organisations, promoting feelings of disillusionment and ***despair***. Why? First, because some organisations position progression as an art rather than a science, a mysterious secret that enables them to dodge making promises that they can't fulfil: better to dampen down the expectations of their people, rather than inflate them and disappoint! Second, some leaders regard it as their divine right to exercise total discretion with regards to who gets promoted, where and when. They jealously guard their promotional patronage – even though it might lead to accusations of bias, nepotism and favouritism – because it bolsters their sense of absolute power, enabling them to get 'their' people in place who, as a result of this largesse, will display devoted and unwavering loyalty *to them*.

By contrast, great service organisations are characterised by meritocratic, transparent and equitable progression and development systems. They are open about what it takes to make it to each level within the organisation, clearly prescribing the necessary skills, competencies, professional accreditation and performance criteria that are required in order to facilitate progression from one level to the next. And they not only do this at junior levels: they are also quite clear about what they require for senior positions. This is important. Research has consistently shown that internal promotions (especially at a senior level within organisations) have far better outcomes – in terms of stability and performance – than external hires. For sure, organisations require a sprinkling of external talent at times to plug capability gaps or resolve latent capacity issues – but by and large, promoting people from within who understand the culture and 'know how to get things done around here' is likely to be far more successful. Consistently promoting from within also sends out a strong signal that people have a strong chance of fulfilling their career aspirations with the organisation they are with, rather than looking outside for advancement opportunities. But how do we suggest that organisations fuel feelings of aspiration and hope amongst their people? In line with what we've just said, they need to delineate clear progression paths, align professional development programmes accordingly and offer practical job transition opportunities backed up with targeted mentoring and on-the-job coaching.

- **Clear progression paths** – as we have already hinted, organisations – who want high retention rates, 'low intention to quit' employee engagement scores, a quality talent pipeline and robust succession plan – need to have transparent progression paths clearly signposted within the organisation. Not only does it provide its people with tangible opportunities to make their dreams a reality; it also frees the company up, enabling it to plan for expansion and growth. What do we regard as key success factors in this area?

  o **Defined 'job families'** – given the multitude of roles and functions, it is essential that organisations make a genuine effort to cross match generic skills requirements across what might seem to be completely different roles to create job families. This will enable them, firstly, to prevent a silo mentality from occurring and, secondly, broaden their talent pool options.

  o **Denominated routes** – however, within each function – operations, for instance – progression routes should be clearly expressed. For instance: team member > team leader > section head > assistant/deputy > general manager > area manager > retail director > operations director etc. In keeping with our first point, however, 'branch routes' that illustrate options that fit into generic job families are also specified (e.g. assistant/deputy > pre-opening trainer, general manager > stock taker, area manager > HR business partner etc.) are extremely informative and motivational.

  o **Pre-specified requirements** – obviously each role requires a job specification but, more importantly, organisations need to outline how individuals can acquire the necessary experience, skills and competencies to *successfully compete for it*.

  o **Transparent measurement and selection** – but ultimately progression paths will be judged on one thing only, namely: the fairness and openness of the job selection process. How are candidates who fulfil the mandatory application requirements judged and measured for the role? How robust are the interviewing and assessment methods? What are the feedback mechanisms for those that fall short at this stage? What remedial development is on offer so that they are successful the next time around?

- **Professional development programmes** – in addition to the path, it goes without saying that organisations should have a suite of professional programmes that facilitate progression from one level to the next. We have talked previously about cognitive, technical and behavioural programmes that 'weaponise' staff to *do* their roles, but here we are concerned with interventions that help individuals progress *to* the next level. Here – in our view – are the main features of their success:

  ○ *Professionally accredited and certified* – wherever possible courses and programmes need to be nationally accredited (in the UK that means certified against Level 1-7 learning outcomes). We have made this point before but it needs repeating. Individuals are far more likely to value the programmes they are on and 'stay the course' if they perceive that the learning they are engaged in increases their professional status and employability. Too often companies offer in-house courses that – as well designed as they are – don't mean anything to other employers. This means that they will lack perceived portability and transference. It is far better for companies to get their courses externally validated and accredited to meet national levels of learning attainment, so that they carry extra weight and external credibility.

  ○ *Preferred learning style 'fit'* – in addition to ensuring that programmes and courses are, as far as possible, linked to nationally accredited and certificated standards, attention must also be paid to ensuring that programme material fits with employee learning styles. What do we mean by this? Most research on knowledge transference and preferred learning has concluded that people are able to absorb information at a different rate, according to which approach is deployed: 'hearing and doing' results in a 70% knowledge retention rate, 'seeing and listening' 40% and 'hearing' 20%! Also, learning in groups is proven to be far more successful than solo learning, as people can provide one another with mutual support and swap ideas. This means that companies have to work harder than just introducing a broad sweep of 'sheep-dip' online programmes, where individuals are expected to work alone to understand and absorb dry information. In service industries, in particular, where employees are behaviourally attuned to displaying dynamic momentum, a combination of (quickly) listening, seeing, doing and reflecting will lead to the effective absorption of information.

- **Transitional mechanisms** – in addition to educational and skills programmes that help individuals bridge the gaps as they progress through an organisation, careful thought must also be given to *how* staff transition into new roles. Too often people are flung into roles to plug unforeseen gaps and are expected to sink or swim with a minimum of prior immersion and exposure. Organisations that softly transition talent into new roles through planned taster secondments, shadowing, 'strawberry' assignments (same job but less responsibility etc.) are far more likely to set people up for success. Gradual and purposeful exposure rather than immediate, panic-stricken immersion will benefit both the individual and organisation in both the shorter and longer term. But our main point is this. Churchill once said that "the only way you can learn to fight is fight!" Transitioning people into new roles does not mean that organisations can send just them on a course in order to be 'fit to fight'. Combat readiness is derived from direct exposure to the stresses, strains and requirements of an unfamiliar position (however well they 'knew how to do it' beforehand). Gradual immersion reduces 'transition shock', enabling individuals to understand what the reality means rather than how the paper specification described it, in terms of effort and focus. It also provides an opportunity for some to admit – after managed immersion – that they can't cope with the new role and revert back to their previous positions, without any loss of ego or reputation.

- **Targeted mentoring** – transitioning roles is made easier if organisations also provide what we call 'targeted mentoring'. What is this? *Mentoring* is a means through which *mentors* (usually more senior people who have run the gamut) can impart knowledge, expertise and experience to mentees (individuals who require transitional advice or general development). It works best when it is *targeted*. That is to say, when the chemistry between the two parties is right, the mentee genuinely feels that they can learn something from their nominated mentor, conversations are structured around tangible issues, challenges and obstacles the mentee is seeking to overcome *and* the mentor is sufficiently mature and sagacious not to constantly lapse into 'when I did' mode! Mentoring also provides an opportunity for mentees to extend their social network and air cover as they develop their careers. In our view, it is an absolutely critical support mechanism for highly aspirational women who might lack self-confidence that they are good enough to succeed in male-dominated environments; and it can enable them (in the absence of a fully developed network) to bond with a potential sponsor and cheerleader in furtherance of their career development. We advise that, prior to their first interactions, mentors be given some guidance on meeting, listening and the asking of probing questions, so that they can supervise their sessions effectively. Too often, mentors are nominated and launched into the process without the requisite skills or understanding as to what their role requires. Likewise, mentees must be made aware of the limitations and ethical boundaries of the process.

- **On-the-job coaching** – whilst mentoring involves the direct transference of expertise, coaching is a process in which the coach (sometimes line manager, other manager or external consultant) raises levels of *awareness* and *accountability* amongst coachees by getting *them* to specify and solve the problems they face *themselves*. It is based on the premise that the answers we seek to problems often lie in ourselves or within our orbit of control. The next section, 'eMOTION #2 – Courageous Coaching', will go into coaching techniques in more detail – particularly with regards to re-framing or shifting coachee perspectives and emotions through 'magic questions'. But often, managers adopting the coach role will use models, such as the GROW model, to help coachees confront and solve issues themselves. With regards to career development and progression, these will involve questions such as:

o ***Goal definition*** – what is your career objective? When do you want to achieve it by? What do you want from me?

o ***Reality of situation*** – what is happening now? On a scale of one to ten, where are you now? What are the major constraints to you finding a way forwards? What is the evidence for that? What would you advise a friend to do if they were in your shoes?

o ***Options for resolution*** – what options do you have? What would be your first step? What else could you do? What would you do differently now?

o ***Will to get it done*** – what are you going to do? When are you going to do it? On a scale of one to ten, what is the likelihood of success? How do you make it a ten? Who needs to know? What support do you need?

This coaching mechanism is particularly useful during career discussions - especially personal development reviews. Why? Because very often individuals look to their line manager or company for solutions, when they should take ownership for driving their own careers. Some organisations will provide ample opportunities for development and progression: it is down to the individual to cast off any inhibitions or bulldoze through any perceived barriers to forge a path for themselves. Also the fact that most coaching models start with nouns such as goal, objective and aim makes the medium suitable for professional development chats (see our BUILD–RAISE coaching model in the next section, 'eMOTION #2 – Courageous Coaching').

In summary, companies that seek to fulfil people's *hopes* and *aspirations* through enriching career development will undoubtedly reap the benefits. As we have said, through signposting clear progression paths backed up with high-value professional programmes, plus coaching and mentoring mechanisms that help individuals to transition roles *and* make the right choices, companies will benefit from higher levels of stability and competence, thus freeing up the firm's capacity for growth. Companies often cite a lack of talent when they fail to fulfil their ambitions but often it is not that they lack talent per se; rather they lack the progression mechanisms to convert what they have got into 'higher grade material'. Organisations who think that they can just buy in talent to grow are often mistaken: investing in the people that have already been hired, onboarded and trained is a far more effective and cost-efficient way of building latent capacity. In addition, we would say two further things. First, companies should make sure that career development meetings are decoupled from annual performance discussions: the former are too important to be conflated and confused with the latter. Second, career discussions should not only feature 'upwards' discussions. There are many key individuals in organisations that have no aspiration to move upwards but could do with a degree of 'refreshment'. There are others for whom moving across an organisation (to gain more insight and experience) is a necessary precursor to moving onwards. Therefore organisations need to give line managers a range of options and mechanisms not only to accelerate careers but also to enrich them. And when people are successful in moving to exciting new opportunities, whether up or across, their *successes should be exclaimed* and communicated across the organisation, a vital process that will be discussed in the next section.

CASE STUDY 15 – **SIMON LONGBOTTOM, CEO, STONEGATE PUB COMPANY**

Simon leads Stonegate – the UK's leading drinks-led managed pub company (with circa 700 pubs and bars) – which has consolidated the high-street segment of the market by making a number of game-changing acquisitions over the past few years. Previously he was Managing Director of Greene King Pub Partnerships and Managing Director of the Gala Gaming Group.

What is my philosophy on career development, *how* do we turn this into practice and *why* is it important?

- **Philosophy** – my philosophy and that of the senior leaders in this company is simple (and we talk about it all the time!):

  o *Bar to boardroom* – it is our sincere belief that anybody has the opportunity to go from the BAR TO THE BOARDROOM in this company. This is backed up by the fact that three out of the four senior leaders have achieved this *exact* feat within this industry.

  o *Home grown* – we believe that growing our own people (who 'get' our purpose, culture and systems) is far more preferable than buying in talent. We have set a target that, by 2019, 90 per cent of all managerial appointments in Stonegate will come from internal sources.

○ **Meritocratic** – we strongly subscribe to the fact that all our appointments should be made fairly and transparently according to merit and achievement rather than favouritism or patronage.

○ **Enriching lives** – we are in the business of enriching our people's lives both monetarily and experientially, if they have a real *aspiration* to move up the career ladder.

- **Practice** – this philosophy is underpinned by tangible practices:

○ **Clear progression paths** – before I arrived we already had a retail career path in place called 'Albert's Theory of Progression'. This shows people how they can build their careers from team member to director in 'bite-sized' chunks. Over the past three years 'Albert' has won thirteen major awards, recognising its impact and effectiveness.

○ **Effective transitional mechanisms** – two of the most challenging career steps within our business are deputy to GM and GM to area manager. So how do we transition talent from one level to the next? In the case of deputy to GM we have our *Accelerator Programme* which equips ambitious young deputies with the appropriate leadership and commercial skills to progress to GM. It has been very successful. We have transitioned 115 managers through the programme to date with an estimated £3m EBITDA dividend (when you compare the performance of this group to a control group which hasn't been through the programme). This excites the CFO and certainly gets his support! We celebrated the work we are doing here by holding a reception for Accelerator graduates (many of whom were under the age of 30) at the House of Commons in November 2016. This generated great PR and publicity for us with regards to the work we are doing with young people. In relation to GM to area manager transitions, we provide mentoring, expert coaching, sideways roles (to grow management and commercial skills) and tailored personal development plans to smooth the path for people.

o **Accredited programmes** – at area management level, I have supported university-accredited multi-unit leadership post-graduate programmes both here at Stonegate and at my previous role at Greene King. Why? When I started in the industry, area management was treated as a dark art but I believe it to be more of a science... involving distributed leadership, precise commercial execution and the generation of genuine hospitality behaviours. This course gives our area managers a framework but also – most crucially – it encourages them to think more like senior managers, it gives them a sense of perspective, a range of coping strategies, a portable qualification *and* it confers a greater sense of self-confidence (both in front of more senior people and in their decision-making processes). Also – and this is the *magical* part – it gives the graduates of the programme an opportunity to take their family to a *memorable* event: a graduation ceremony, which recognises their immense achieve-ment in gaining a highly valued postgraduate qualification.

- **Importance** – why do I believe that this is all so important?

    o **Commercial benefit** – we have proven (especially through our Accelerator analysis) that investment in this area enhances skills and capabilities, giving Stonegate real bang for our buck. This is not a soft intervention done for well-intentioned purposes: it has hard commercial outcomes!
    o **Personal experience** – as the beneficiary of transitional programmes that have progressed me 'from the bar to the boardroom', I am a passionate advocate of their success.
    o **Discretionary effort** – hospitality is 24/7. It is a tough industry. If you want to generate discretionary effort that results in great service outcomes, you *must* invest in your people. I am a great believer in the Service Profit Chain concept – indeed, I put it up at all of the presentations I give to our teams. We have to build the *emotional bank account* amongst our people. We have to 'give out' and show *we* care about them. They, in turn, will 'give back' and care about our customers! And that is the way to build a successful and sustainable business.

Enrich Careers (generating HOPE) – Five Key Points

- Signpost progression paths
- Build effective career transition mechanisms
- Externally accredit and certify development programmes
- Provide targeted mentoring and career coaching
- Build the capability of 'stars' *and* 'pillars'

---

9. EXCLAIM SUCCESSES – Communicate (Generating PRIDE)

The ninth moment of emotional truth for organisations in the employment cycle is open and vibrant communications which create a feeling of belonging and *pride* by exclaiming successes and shaping purposeful behaviours. Honest communications serve a vital role in building trust and engagement within companies, also serving as a vehicle to reinforce key messages through showcasing 'what good looks like'. Often in organisations, individuals complain that they don't know what is really going on and that they don't trust the 'corporate spin' that is peddled down the line. They treat what they are being told with *cynicism* and scepticism because the rhetoric they are being fed is so far from their everyday reality. In short, communications is viewed as a form of corporate propaganda, which – given the plethora of other digital channels they can surf to uncover the true story – is consistently undermined by what they find out elsewhere. Unlike the pre-digital age when companies could manage their narrative, today employees have several means through which they can uncover the unspun truth. The only way organisations can counter this (which is difficult for managers stuck in the old 'controlled media' paradigm) is to give people the unbridled truth, whilst paying heed to their legal and fiduciary responsibilities. For, at times – it must be said – companies cannot tell the full story (particularly with regards to market-sensitive information)! However, we would argue that organisations can strike a balance here and, at the very least, be clear with their people what they can and can't tell them publically and attempt to fill in the blanks through other 'private' means (i.e. confidential one-to-one briefings of classified information).

Our point is this. In order for communications systems to work, there has to be a widespread feeling amongst people that what they are being told is believable. If this is the case, they can then use these channels to motivate, inspire and engender *pride* amongst their people. Excepting this need for a solid reputation for truth, then, what do we believe are the main facets of successful communications? We would point to the following 'content' and 'process' factors: impactful *key* messages driven through a coherent multi-channel approach, accompanied by robust, trackable feedback systems.

- **KEY messages and imagery** – internal communications systems are successful when they hammer home consistent messages: those that constantly reinforce the *purpose*, *principles* and *practice* of the organisation. They are bolstered further when external communications and imagery are similarly aligned (i.e. when the messages that shareholders and customers receive chime with what is being said internally). This avoids the pitfalls and dangers of mixed signalling which might confuse and disorientate employees. But internally, what are the key messages that successful organisations must transmit?

  - *Financial performance and growth* – first of all company members need to know how the organisation is performing. Why? Because policy makers should understand that most people process information in terms of what it might *mean to them*. That is to say communicators must always address the '*what's in it for me?*' and '*how does this affect my position?*' questions. At a basic level most people want to know that they are safe and secure in their jobs; so to this extent, communications must give an honest appraisal of financial performance. If good – fine – most individuals will go about their jobs safe in the knowledge that their company has momentum. If bad, people will want to know what plans the organisation has in place to get back onto a *growth path* that protects their own personal positions. Sometimes this will, inevitably, include some negative news (in terms of job cuts and closures): but as long as these announcements are handled sensitively, accompanying actions are *humane and swift* and underlying rationale is sound (i.e. a return to growth), 'surviving' staff will be more inclined to swing behind the organisation.

o *KPI achievement* – the financial performance of an organisation will usually be accompanied by a plethora of KPIs (financial, operational, customer and employee) some of which are accompanied by bonuses and incentives. Regular updates on performance against these KPIs are crucial, because people are more inclined to manage what they are being measured against. We would make two points here. First, the closer these KPIs are fitted to what people can control in their daily lives the better (i.e. according to team, shift and unit). Second, they should have reasonably short achievement timescales, so that behaviour is 'animated' on a regular basis. Too often, KPIs are detached from what individuals can control on the ground and are beset by complicated, unwieldy hurdles and timelines. 'Close', controllable and timely KPIs work best.

o *Initiatives and improvements* – performance and KPI information is crucial to people's sense of wellbeing and motivation but this data - once it is communicated - is often backward looking. What about the future? What is the organisation doing to forge a successful path ahead? What exciting initiatives and improvements to operations and/or the offer will give people confidence that the company is investing for success? Here, leaders must be careful that they don't exaggerate too much by making overblown claims and statements about operational improvement mechanisms (e.g. IT upgrades and reporting procedures) that either fail to live up to their original billing as making life easier or that are actually wolves in sheep's clothing (e.g. draconian cost-cutting initiatives hidden behind a narrative of improvement). Indeed, we would suggest that the upsides and potential downsides of all 'efficiency' initiatives need to be explained honestly, moderating expectations from the off. The improvement initiatives that people most like to hear about - those that are targeted at sales growth - should be similarly positioned: although people will be far more inclined to willingly line up behind these initiatives!

o *Uplifting success stories* – accompanying all this vital information which keeps people attuned to how the organisation is doing and what its future growth plans are, uplifting vignettes and examples of individual success stories are required to create potent imagery. Of course, the Soviet Union was a master of this, highlighting the 'Stakhanovite' successes of workers who, in the glorious furtherance of the motherland, (allegedly) achieved prodigious agricultural, coal mining and iron-ore smelting productivity feats. We certainly aren't suggesting that organisations go this far, fabricating heroic stories of success 'pour encourager les autres'. But by highlighting *genuine* individual and team successes (i.e. performance, promotion, training/development achievement, innovation etc.) the company not only reinforces what it is trying to achieve and models the desired behaviours it requires, it also lifts people's spirits and sense of ambition.

- **Coherent multi-channel approach** – but how should vital messages and information be conveyed? Which channels are best suited? Our view is that different media suit different messages:

  - *Face-to-face* – there is a creeping orthodoxy that holds that digital is best for *all* forms of communication these days, given that millennials, in particular, spend a disproportionate amount of time checking or using their smartphone devices (and with 80 per cent of the UK adult population owning one). In spite of this, we still hold that some communication is best conducted face-to-face. Any announcement that might affect jobs *must* be made face-to-face, so that managers can 'front up' on any direct questions. Only disorganised, heartless corporate entities choose to impart such information 'down the wire'; the long-term ramifications for which (in terms of trust and morale) can be severe. In short, face-to-face briefings are useful for cascaded information that requires *deep* rather than *surface* explanation.

  - *Digital 'pulse briefings'* – but, given as we've said, people today are far more used (or 'addicted') to getting their information through online smartphone technology, organisations increasingly use 'pulse briefings' on a range of issues to keep their people up-to-date with company developments and progress. Such methods also enable policy makers to get a tighter grip on communications given the fact that – in spite of mandatory policy – some managers fail to hold regular staff meetings or follow the 'corporate brief' when they hold them! Such channels minimise the chances that people are kept in the dark about what's happening (though middle managers deliberately hoarding information to reinforce their power and authority) ensuring companies can get over the *right information, to the right people at the right time*.

- ○ **Social-media platforms** – obviously many companies and their managers have made great use of 'open' and 'closed' social-media platforms to disseminate information, particularly in video format. These real-time visual communication channels are a great way of showcasing and celebrating success, as well as sparking up conversations and dialogue amongst participants. They create social communities of practice and knowledge, leveraging the wider talents of the team. These media (such as Facebook and Yammer) are sure to evolve over time, developing exciting new applications that managers can leverage, although the security of the sites and maturity of the participants are fundamental prerequisites of their reliability and sustainability.

- *Two-way feedback mechanisms* – as technology improves at an exponential rate, managers are able to communicate at a distance through FaceTime, video conferencing, Skype and webinar mechanisms. This enables them not only to convey information but also to harness the views and insights of their teams in an open environment. Again, it enables them to ask their teams the vital question: what should we start, stop or continue doing in order to sustain or improve things? To this extent, there has never been a better environment for leaders to connect directly with team members that they might only have seen or interacted with on an extremely infrequent basis. However – as always – it is not the process that is the most important catalyst in moving things forward, it is whether or not leaders actually *listen* to and act upon – rather than just *hear* and ignore – what they are being told!

In summary, organisations that communicate *effectively* with their people consistently get their tone, content and channels right. Their core messages and updates are conveyed as honestly and transparently as possible, enlivened by positive imagery and uplifting stories of success that generate intense feelings of *pride* and belonging. We would offer two further insights. First – due to the all-pervasive influence of the Internet – the days of tightly managed communications are over, meaning companies must have quick response mechanisms in place to react to unjustified rumour and negative stories. If at times they cannot control the agenda, they must have systems in place whereby they can quickly scotch falsehoods and lies. To this extent senior people must be 'weaponised' with the requisite tools and advice to prevent their messages from being derailed by external forces. Second, CEOs can no longer detach themselves from communicating, insisting – as many of them did in the past – that apparatchiks from the comms department do all their dirty work for them. Due to the new digital paradigm, communications has moved into the C-suite and is now a prime responsibility of the CEO. Recently a hospitality CEO remarked to us that during his store visits he was disappointed to find that his people just didn't get it with regards to strategy and operational excellence. When asked whether he communicated his business imperatives across the business through regular video messages and updates – like so many of his contemporaries do today – he remarked:"that's not my job, that's what I pay my MDs and Operations Directors to do!" Six months later, he was out of a job.

CEOs and the leaders of organisations have unparalleled opportunities to access channels which enable them to *transmit* powerful messages directly to all their employees: there is no excuse for ignoring them in this day and age. Even better, they can also use them to *receive* and process vital information and feedback! This will help them to calibrate and *evaluate* the mood, capability and performance within their organisation, something that will be examined in the next section.

CASE STUDY 16 – **RUFUS HALL, MANAGING DIRECTOR, FINE FOOD CAPITAL (EX-CEO, ORCHID GROUP)**

Rufus Hall is the former CEO of the Orchid Group which he and his team sold to Mitchells and Butlers for an industry-leading price of £266m in 2014. Rufus is widely regarded as having played a pivotal role in turning Orchid around during challenging economic circumstances (when many operators folded) and extreme competitive pressures. He is currently Managing Director, Fine Food Capital UK. A veteran of the food-service sector, he previously held senior roles at Tom Cobleigh, Ha! Ha!, Punch and S&N Retail.

The components of any successful (profitable) food-service brand must incorporate three fundamental components: comfortable environment, great people and quality products. But it is the people that make the real difference. It is a simple equation really: *happy staff who are proud to work in a brand = happy customers who are proud to recommend the brand*! That was our mission at Orchid and I think we achieved it. We were certainly nationally recognised for doing so and our new owners paid us the highest compliment when they said that they wanted to incorporate a number of key elements of our culture. But I must emphasise this: it was *not about money*. It didn't cost us a great deal. So how did we go about it? How did we make our people feel *proud*?

- **Clear vision, mission and values** – the starting point was our vision, mission and values. When we embarked on putting these together, I was fairly sceptical about this stuff but, in retrospect, they really worked. They really were the glue that bound us together.
  - *Vision* – 'Make everyone feel part of the family'
  - *Mission* – 'To grow a profitable company where our people are proud to work and our customers are proud to recommend us'
  - *Values* –
    - Be a real part of your community
    - Respect every £ we spend
    - Continually challenge the status quo
    - Attract and nurture the very best people
    - Create an enjoyable place to work
    - Always deliver exceptional standards and service

- **Aligned communication** – what we did was weave these values into all the messages we conveyed to staff. But, fundamentally, they were brought to life in two main ways:
  - Through a *newspaper* that was frequently circulated amongst staff. It was written in a fun, tabloid way to communicate to everyone. It kept communicating and celebrating examples that demonstrated how we were living the values...
  - Via *performance appraisals* and business development discussions which were framed around the core values. Measuring people against the values changed behaviours! 'What gets measured, gets managed. What gets managed, gets, done!'

- **Opportunity, recognition and fun** – in addition, we put together fabulous training programmes (that won several awards) and provided career development opportunities. We also made a point of encouraging all our leaders to recognise the small things that people did on a day-to-day basis. We worked hard on making Orchid a fun place to work: doing spontaneous things that brought both joy and excitement to our people on the ground!

- **External accreditation** – our efforts to create an environment which fostered a sense of pride and engagement were recognised by the *Sunday Times'* 100 Best Companies to Work For, Publican Awards, Investors in People and Scotland's Best Employer Awards. These awards not only recognised the hard work we had put into building a vibrant, happy and profitable company but strengthened our employment brand. It enhanced the feelings of pride that people had working for us and made us more attractive to prospective staff.

- **Tangible benefits** – as I said: *happy staff = happy customers = we make money*! It didn't cost us a lot but our staff stability rates increased (people stayed longer) and it made recruitment easier. Also our emphasis on fun and challenging the status quo made it a very enjoyable place to work. When we were bought by our new owners, they stated publically that they wanted to learn from and incorporate elements of our unique company culture! But in the end, when I reflect back, our people were proud to work for Orchid. And I am proud of that fact.

CASE STUDY 17 – **PATRICIA THOMAS, EX-OPERATIONS DIRECTOR, DOMINO'S PIZZA GROUP**

Patricia Thomas is an industry-leading franchise consultant having previously been Director of International Development and Executive Director of Operations of Domino's Pizza Group (DPG) UK. Previously, she held senior positions with Domino's (US) following stints at the Michel's Baguette French Bakery Café franchise and Houlihan's Restaurants.

[At the start of our Operational Quality Transformation Programme at Domino's] I started to work on our relationships with our franchisees by having informal meals and drinks with many of them, bringing them back into balance (overcoming objections and problem raising) by recognising their contribution... asking about *how* they had got here today – listening to their stories, which almost served as a conscious reminder to them *why* what they were doing was important...We also set up *regular calendar communications events* which were designed to inform franchisees honestly and directly what we were doing, *seeking their advice and buy-in* to changes... The message that I relentlessly conveyed during these interactions was that we had to get better at executing the brand... I used my experiences in the US as a powerful anecdote to highlight how operations that lose focus on product quality and speed of delivery can 'drift off'... but what I also did was to empirically demonstrate a financial link between investing in staff training, deployment and equipment, their positive effects upon operational execution and customer satisfaction/sales out-turns. I used live examples of operators that had good Operational Evaluation Reviews (OER) and speed of delivery scores that had translated great sales figures (this had never been done before)... showing that investing in your business really pays off. To ensure constancy of purpose we also tied OERs and delivery times into specific targets with related rewards and consequences... At the same time the company introduced real-time comparative (store vs store) delivery data that showed up on FOH EPOS systems at store level and invested heavily in digital ordering systems... the cost for which was shared between the company and the franchisees...

The net impact of all these changes was a dramatic improvement in operational execution... OER scores moved from 3.53 stars on a 5-star scale to 4.27 stars – the highest achievement of any market in the Domino's system. During this period of time, average sales per unit grew by 47% and the number of stores in the UK and Ireland grew by 62%... but – as I said – the way we drove these changes was by fundamentally improving our relationships with our franchisees: not through formal committees (where members can sometimes be driving their own agendas) – but by *one-to-one, face-to-face communications* where we both listened and got our message over... reminding franchisees about the 'why', instilling a sense of pride... selling the financial benefits of 'doing it right' and providing extra data/support to make it happen... One further thought I would add is that, given the transitory nature of much franchisor management, it is important that operational *transformation is led by inspirational leaders with credibility who really monitor 'the incentive to perform' and care about franchisee profit*... winning franchisors make 'good' sustainable profit rather than 'bad' short-termist gains...

10. EVALUATE AND EVOLVE – Review (Generating GRATITUDE)

Thus far, this book has examined nine 'emotional moments of truth' that inspirational leaders need to address in order to ensure organisational success. We have argued that, at every stage, effectiveness is achieved by leaders who consciously seek to make their employees and customers employees *feel positive and uplifted*. Hence, at every stage of the employment cycle, we have drawn attention to the *purpose*, *principles* and *practices* of inspirational leaders that have drawn the best out of their direct reports and wider teams. But organisations do not exist in a vacuum. Although the company they lead might have achieved primacy or first-mover advantage in their particular sector, their competitive set will be breathing down their neck. The competitive advantage they have carved out through having a dynamic purpose, vibrant culture and motivated workforce might begin to be eroded by competitors who have caught up, either through imitation or innovation. Very often organisations are caught off guard by this 'competitive creep', believing that what they have done in the past to be successful will be enough to maintain their success in the future. This is arrogant and misguided but not at all uncommon. Why? Often leaders are caught napping at the wheel because they are too lazy, complacent and incurious to refresh their proposition, processes and practices. Also, they are incapable of learning new approaches that will fit with new commercial paradigms or are unprepared to 'unlearn' approaches that don't! This is deadly. Research by one of the world's leading executive search companies, Korn Ferry International, looked at a number of contingent variables connected to leader effectiveness, concluding that capacity to learn was the most important attribute connected with sustained executive success.

This fits with our view. The best service organisations are nearly always led by who leaders who we call 'Evolvers' (or in extreme cases 'Revivers') – individuals who demonstrate a passion and relentless urge to learn and absorb how to do things better and faster in order to drive performance to new levels. Sometimes this will entail killing off sacred cows that people in the organisation had previously protected in the (misguided) belief that they were unnegotiable, crucial foundations of success. More often, Evolver leaders need to get the organisation back on track by returning an organisation that has drifted away from its original purpose and principles *back to its 'true north'*, whilst simultaneously updating and refreshing its offer and systems. Such actions will sweep aside misgivings and **apprehension**, generating feelings of **gratitude** and increased confidence amongst their staff. But how they do this? How do Evolvers sustain or regain organisational traction? How do they ensure – as we pointed out right at the beginning (Moment of Truth 1 – 'Evocative Experience') – that their employees and customers *love* working and transacting with them? Essentially, by constantly *evaluating* and *evolving* both their people and product (its *proposition, operational execution* and *culture*). These will now be examined in turn.

- **Evaluate and evolve people** – inspirational leaders must have performance review systems in place which enable people to know how they are performing and where they stand. These will (largely) promote feelings of relief and thankfulness amongst staff, *most* of whom want to be perceived as doing a good job. It is also an opportunity for inspirational leaders to have honest conversations with people who are not cutting it, suggesting that great opportunities lie for them elsewhere. How? Through regular formal performance appraisals and coaching, plus – most importantly – informal ad hoc discussions which reduce levels of fear and anxiety amongst self-critical high performers that they aren't doing as well as they should. The next section, 'eMOTION #2 – Courageous Coaching', will address in depth how inspirational leaders evolve their people's capability and performance through coaching and mentoring.

- **Evolve proposition** - in order to remain relevant, cutting edge and *loved*, Evolvers must constantly evaluate and evolve their organisation's core proposition through:

- ○ ***Researching trends and relevance*** – the first thing that Evolvers must do is evaluate big-data feedback and trends. What are customers *spontaneously* saying about the experience their brand provides on social media sites? What are they saying about the 'happening' brands in their sector? As a result they ask the following questions with regards to both imitating and shaping: what are the happening brands in our segment doing that we're not? What can we imitate or bastardise immediately without compromising the integrity of our positioning? How can we shape the segment going forwards? How do we leverage developing consumer preferences and tastes to our own advantage? How can we sustain/restore our reputation for category leadership and innovation?

- ○ ***Asking the right people, the right questions*** – in addition to harvesting spontaneous remarks, Evolvers must also ask questions – *but the right ones to the right people!* Brands commonly ask *existing* users satisfaction questions relating to quality, speed of service, propensity to recommend (e.g. NPS) and so forth but they often miss out the views and opinions of *lapsed* and *non-users*. Evolvers must seek their views! Also – as we have argued elsewhere in this book – Evolvers must consult *their teams* i.e. the people who are capable of offering the most telling insights and advice. How? Frontline staff who are in frequent daily contact with customers (i.e. GMs and service providers) should be asked: *if you had the autonomy to change one thing that would improve the customer experience, what would you do?* In addition, Evolvers should glean information from other stakeholders that have a valid perspective on the brand's performance/future direction such as suppliers, shareholders and (where applicable) franchisees.

- ○ ***Reinvigorating benefits*** – having looked at nascent trends and established what a range of constituents think, the Evolver must now cheerlead functional and emotional enhancements to the brand. Bearing in mind what people have said and what the Evolver intuitively feels will work, (s)he must address the following questions: what enhancements to the brand can we (quickly) make now that will be of high perceived value to employees and customers (but low cost to us!)? Is the brand's value proposition (i.e. price, product quality, service and environment) imbalanced and, if so, what elements need fixing now? What changes can we make – in accordance with the core purpose and principles of this brand – to make our employees and customers *love* us again (or to sustain their love)? What changes can we make to the marketing mix that will make us stand out from the crowd once again? The Evolver will know that (s)he is succeeding if the changes to recapture the original buzz and excitement energise employees (resulting in higher staff retention and employee opinion survey scores) and cause customers to react with enthusiasm (mirrored in higher Net Promoter scores and spontaneous advocacy on social media sites).

o *Diverging rather than converging* – but there is one thing that successful Evolvers achieve through their process of evaluation and evolution, namely, as we said in our previous book: be different and stay different – or perish! There is a tendency amongst some leaders to look to other concepts for inspiration. There is nothing wrong with this: at the very least, competitive parity must be maintained. But successful Evolvers must try to ensure that their brand continues to be perceived as *innovative*, *fun* and *fresh* rather than mediocre. Average is the enemy of excellence.

- **Evolve operational execution** - evaluating and evolving the proposition must go hand-in-hand with refreshing processes that underpin execution (i.e. structure, systems and monitoring). Organisations must remain nimble and agile to adapt to changing market demands and circumstances. Those that become inert, bureaucratic and ossified will be unable to respond to competitive pressure, eventually (and inevitably) crumbling into the abyss! Thus, Evolvers need to:

o *Review architecture* – the first act of Evolvers during the act of sharpening up processes and execution is to ensure that the architecture of the enterprise is fit for purpose. To this end, they will pose a number of questions. How efficiently is the operation organised, geographically? Are the strategic business units segmented efficiently (i.e. addressing the right markets and customer)? Do they have optimal 'spans of control'? Are the core functions aligned and (where necessary) embedded in the operational line?

- ○ ***Review KPIs and measures*** – with regards to what is being measured by the organisation, the Evolver needs to ask a number of key questions. Are the right behaviours being encouraged by the current KPIs and incentives? Has the organisation prioritised the correct measures to drive assured outcomes? (I.e. is there a focus on profit outputs rather than service/standards inputs?) Are the targets in place too soft (resulting in shirking) or too hard (resulting in poor morale)? Are the KPIs for the organisation cascaded appropriately? Most importantly, do frontline service providers have simple, well-understood SMART objectives that link to the organisations strategic priorities?

- ○ ***Reboot values*** – alongside these 'hard' controls, the Evolver might need to revisit the ideological values of the organisation, asking the following questions: are the values of the organisation still relevant and consistent with what we are trying to achieve as an enterprise? Are the values widely disseminated, understood and modelled within the organisation? Are they shaping and guiding *intentional* and *purposeful* behaviours that add *executional* value to the organisation? If the answers to some of these questions are negative then the Evolver will need to reboot the values system of the organisation through communications, personal example and publically recognising great values-led behaviours. As discussed elsewhere in this book, values systems clearly stating 'the way we do business around here' are one of the main mechanisms that leaders can leverage to bind the organisation together with a sense of common purpose and self-regulating behaviour, resulting in operational excellence. If they have become outdated or fallen into abeyance, the Evolver must reinvigorate the whole values process.

- • **Evolve culture** – lastly, in keeping with the focus of this book, Evolvers must push the envelope by continuing to galvanise and inspire their organisation. Having felt the pulse of their organisation through personal observation and deep evaluation of employee feedback, they set about moving it forwards by reinvigorating the culture. Inevitably they will revisit, analyse and tweak many of the practices we have talked about in this book. But what are the major things they do to revitalise their culture?

  - ○ ***Paint a picture*** – the first thing that the Evolver should do is keep the organisation *alive* to the enormous market opportunity that remains, whilst emphasising the pain that people will have to go through in order to crystallise it. The leader must cast a narrative spell over his/her followers with a compelling vision for the future of the brand. This is more effectively achieved through stories that paint a picture of the 'promised land' destination, making the discomfort of the journey seem somehow palatable, rather than just dry, rational explanations and numbers.

○ **Potent symbolism** – in order to demonstrate momentum, the Evolver can take a number of quick actions that will symbolise the fact that 'things are going to be kept dynamic around here'. If the organisation is morphing into a bureaucracy, (s)he can immediately set the new tone by despatching decisions swiftly and holding brief, purposeful meetings where people are held *individually* to account for what has been agreed collectively. Instant reductions in, and removal of, hierarchy, deference and status will also have a profound effect on staff *feelings* regarding fairness, equity and openness. Evolver leaders never underestimate the potency of making quick symbolic changes that, first, signal the way in which they want business to be professionally transacted and, second, set the behavioural foundations for major transformational change further down the line.

○ **Eliminate saboteurs** – but in order to reinvigorate the culture, the Evolver will also have to take some tough decisions, smoking out and despatching individuals intent on derailing their change process. Generally there are four types of resistors in organisations: protestors (who openly declare their opposition to change), zombies (who have no opinions of their own and are easily led by opponents of change), survivors (who maintain a self-interested strategy of 'malevolent silence') and saboteurs (who covertly conspire and undermine). Of these categories, the *saboteurs* are the most dangerous because they wilfully (and secretly) scheme to block and derail any changes that threaten their own position or the status quo. In order to flush out this enemy and in addition to monitoring behaviours, the Evolver must examine hard outcomes. Where is the change being blocked, halted or diluted? By whom and when? (S)he must then act decisively to remove malevolent *saboteurs* from the 'field of play'.

o ***Demonstrate personal sacrifice*** – but the main thing that resets the cultural tone is how the Evolver acts personally: demonstrating and enduring *authentic* personal sacrifice, signalling a 'we're all in it together' mentality. By working long hours, expending tremendous amounts of energy and taking little in return (i.e. spurning or redistributing large short-term personal bonuses and incentives), the Evolver inspires genuine followership during the tough tasks and choices that lie ahead. (S)he does not make token-gesture sacrifices that are exposed as opportunistic PR exercises further on down the line (in Annual Report disclosures, for instance) but real sacrifices that are respected and imitated by their team during what can be a tough and brutal process of reinvention and regeneration.

In summary, this section has outlined what we believe to be the last moment of emotional truth, namely: *evaluating and evolving* people, proposition, operational execution and culture. We have argued that this function is done best by Evolver leaders who display a heady mixture of managerial and leadership skills, incorporating those we mentioned in the first section of this book ('Inspirational Leadership Qualities'): spiritualism, holism, proactivity and optimism. What feelings do these actions evoke amongst followers? We believe that they arouse intense feelings of *gratitude*. There is appreciation and thankfulness that the Evolver is attempting to take both individuals and the organisation forwards, rather than letting it slide in the face of ferocious competition and changing customer needs. We would offer two further insights. First, it would be misleading to attribute the success of an enterprise solely to one caricatured individual. This book has focused upon how organisations build residual strength and capability through enlightened people practices that engender *feelings such as love, enthusiasm, excitement and pride*, ensuring it triumphs in both good times and bad. Organisations that have the emotional cornerstones we have outlined in this book will be far more resilient and enduring than those that don't! Second – and connectedly – we would argue that *all* leaders should aspire to be Evolvers, constantly evaluating and stimulating change, because in today's digital world stasis is not an option. Business models are constantly being disrupted by new technologies and, within this new paradigm, consumer preferences and behaviours are changing quickly. However, business leaders who constantly question, review and redefine their *purpose, principles* and *practices* are those that are most likely to succeed in today's environment.

CASE STUDY 18 – **JAMES SPRAGG, CHIEF OPERATING OFFICER, CASUAL DINING GROUP – REJUVENATING CAFÉ ROUGE**

From November 2014 to June 2016, James was the Managing Director of Café Rouge, charged with orchestrating its turnaround from a failing brand to one that could once again grow and compete successfully in the casual dining marketplace. An experienced food-service professional, James had previously been a Director for TGI Friday's, Strada and Pizza Express.

When I came to Café Rouge I found a confused brand of 90 or so sites, populated by employees who didn't believe in what they were doing or where they were going. Previous management – well-meaning as it was – had chopped and changed direction. They had lost track of what the brand was about: I found lots of 'initiatives' but no sustainable plan. This brand was desperate for *leadership*. It needed somebody who was going to stand up for the brand and give it a sense clarity, purpose and direction. So this is what I did with the help of my brand team:

- **Evaluate problem** – the first thing I did was listen to the people closest to the customers. I spent time with the restaurant managers, some of whom had spent 20 years with the brand! I went around the 10 areas and met them in groups, spending two-to-three hours listening to how we had got ourselves into this position and what the potential solutions might be. I combined this with a forensic investigation of a raft of data: general feedback, customer reviews, complaints, internal data (employee engagement, turnover, audit scores etc.).

- **Fix the proposition** – having listened to all stakeholders and looked at the data it was clear that so much had been *done* to the brand. But fundamentally it had drifted off course. We had to get back to basics. This brand started life as an *authentic all-day French bistro*: warmly serving classic, *authentic French food done really well*. It did not exist to opportunistically grow sales by incorporating 'on trend' items such as hotdogs onto the menu: something that the previous regime had done to try to attract a younger audience. We were a 'heritage' rather than a 'cool fashion' brand and we had to go after and delight our core customers. The stats said it all: 53% of our revenue came from the 45–65 demographic, with 36% of total revenue coming from 45–65-year-old females. Heavily vouchering younger traffic through our doors was tantamount to disrespecting and abusing our core loyals. This brand need to be *nurtured*, *protected* and *loved* again: in keeping with its original founding principles. To this end we:

- o ***Fixed the food and drink*** – we focused on delivering fresher, classic French food off a simplified cooking platform. Six menus throughout the estate were reduced to one.
- o ***Invested in the amenity*** – we instigated a BOH and FOH two-year investment programme (which focused on producing '6-star' kitchens) which refreshed the brand and made it more ergonomically efficient.
- o ***Sharpened our promotion*** – we invested in new website technology, driving clearer brand messages to our target customers. Brand partnerships and enhanced PR also drove increased awareness about the fact we were 'back in town' as Britain's *favourite all-day dining bistro* where guests could expect good value French food in a *nice relaxed environment*.

- **Revitalised culture** – in addition, we had to put some emotion back into the brand by getting our people to believe and *care* about what they were doing. We had inherited a situation where we had far too many restaurant manager vacancies and/or inexperienced appointments made from assistant management level. Also staff turnover was far too high. So what did we do? First, we filled the vacancies (initially with external talent) and upskilled our management teams. Second, we engaged the troops through our weekly newsletter celebrating any quick wins and showcasing the achievements of 'Ten Heroes of the Week' from the business. Third, the board and I were visible and *present* in the business: people could see that we *cared* as much as they did about the business and if we *cared* more about our customers than our competitors – we won! For instance, we took customer complaints really seriously and in a fairly short space of time we reduced complaints from 1 in 1,000 meals to 1 in 2,000!

- **Relentless execution** – in order to maintain momentum, we scrutinised a number of key KPIs and metrics to ensure we kept on track. From an input point of view we looked at retention, succession and engagement metrics to monitor employee satisfaction. Making sure that we had stable, well-trained teams that felt engaged and *empowered* was a key component in our success. From an output angle we had weekly mystery customer data that told us whether or not our standards and service steps adherence were up to scratch. But, in addition, I focused the team on the spontaneous feedback from digital message boards like TripAdvisor, which ranked our restaurants within their local areas. In spite of its imperfections, this is what our customers read! Tellingly, our average scores rose from an average of three to over four during the turnaround period (with some restaurants hitting 5/5).

Within 12 months, we returned this brand back into growth. What am I most proud about? First, that we completed a brand turnaround in a period of unprecedented food-service growth and competition. Second, this growth has been sustained since I moved roles to the Group COO position. The brand remains in sales growth and also has recently secured major franchise partners abroad in the Middle East. Third, the fact that we saved an iconic brand – that our customers and staff fundamentally felt proud about – but which could easily have gone the way of other failed brands. This was a team effort involving everyone from the supportive investors who gave funding and the space for it to happen, to the brand support team who set the direction and, of course the most important people, the restaurant managers and their teams who executed the turnaround by looking after their guests and embracing the changes.

Evaluate and Evolve (generating GRATITUDE) – Key Points

- Evaluate personal performance
  a. Formal and ad hoc (praise 'stars')
  b. Develop through courageous conversations
- Evolve...
  a. Proposition: *diverge rather than converge*
  b. Operational execution: *faster, better, more consistently*
  c. Culture: *strengthen and deepen*

Summary

In summary, emotions are the most significant motivator of human actions. Positive emotions at the workplace unleash discretionary effort, creativity and a desire to fulfil customer needs. As such, we have identified ten stages in the employment cycle where inspirational leaders either consciously or unconsciously deploy a number of practices that generate eMOTION: **shifting and moving feelings** from ambivalence to **love,** caution to **desire,** scepticism to **awe,** vulnerability to **confidence,** apathy to **enthusiasm,** exasperation to **joy,** frustration to **trust,** despair to **hope,** cynicism to **pride** and apprehension to **gratitude.** We would offer two further insights. First, we accept that negative emotions can be beneficial: our ability to process negative feelings (i.e. seeing reality with clarity rather than excessive optimism) has been proven to lead to higher levels of resilience and better mental health. Second, humans can cultivate and reposition their emotions from negative to positive and vice versa. However, it is the magic touch of the inspirational leader that mobilises positive eMOTION: *reframing* perspectives, *moving* feelings and *shifting* behaviours to create the conditions for super-performance. But what about moving people and their performance levels through more intimate one-to-one coaching interactions? It is to this that we next turn our attention.

'People don't care how much you know
until you show how much you care…'

Theodore Roosevelt

**eMOTION #2
Courageous Coaching**

Definition and Impact

In the previous section we looked at the practices that inspirational leaders deploy during the Ten Emotional Moments of Truth in the employment cycle. Such practices, we argued 'moved' teams: *mobilising* positivity, *shifting* attitudes and behaviours, *stirring* feelings, *resetting* mindsets and *galvanising* teams into action. In short, creating eMOTION. In a couple of sections (most notably 'ENRICH CAREERS – Develop' and 'EVALUATE AND EVOLVE – Review'), we referred to the critical role that inspirational leaders play in *leader-coach roles*, coaching and mentoring subordinates to higher levels of performance. It is to this critical feature of inspirational leadership practice we return to now.

It is our belief that a key component of the inspirational leader's weaponry is their capacity, as a leader-coach, to master what we call 'courageous coaching'. So, what is this and why is it important? First, our definition of CC:

> courageous coaching takes place in a trusting one-to-one learning context where great leader–coaches help coachees RAISE their self-awareness and BUILD accountability by CHALLENGING self-limiting mindsets, mobilising behavioural change and personal progression…

But what is the significance of each component of this definition?

> *Courageous coaching* – a process in which inspirational leaders drop their 'expert leader' or 'performance management' persona (a courageous act in itself!) to challenge and move false preconceptions of coaches
>
> *Trusting one-to-one learning* – a space outside normal performance reviews where – with no hidden agendas – the focus is purely upon personal development and increased effectiveness
>
> *Great leader–coaches help coachees* – where the leader–coach facilitates and guides a coaching (and mentoring) process designed to improve and progress coachees' goals
>
> *RAISE their self-awareness* – focusing upon uncovering 'blind self' and false preconceptions which might be holding them back
>
> *BUILD accountability* – in order to generate genuine ownership of a clear goal, options to overcome obstacles and a plan of action
>
> *CHALLENGING self-limiting mindsets* – reframing and breaking down misconceptions of limitations and barriers
>
> *Mobilising behavioural change and personal progression* – leading to lasting behavioural change and sustainable progress

Figure 3 **Courageous Coaching Definition**

Further on, we will outline tools and strategies that great leader–coaches use during courageous coaching, but – to answer the second question – why is courageous coaching so important? We believe it is important for a number of reasons: some which relate to individual and others to organisational performance.

- **Enhanced individual performance** – from our extensive experience of coaching and mentoring, those that have been exposed to our courageous coaching process (CCP) often comment that they have a greater ability to *solve problems, make better decisions, acquire new skills, think more creatively, manage stress and anxiety more effectively* and *reach career goals* due to increased:

  - *Clarity* – CCP brings focus and value-added prioritisation (big rocks) as it begins with establishing (credible) aims and goals for coaches

  - *Meaning and purpose* – as CCP is forward looking, progressive and focused upon advancement (rather than being backward looking and retrospective), it brings a sense of meaning and purpose to coaches

o *Learning and unlearning* – CCP also provides a valuable space for coachees to contemplate change and new ways of addressing what might previously have seemed to be insurmountable obstacles

o *Positive mindsets and behaviours* – this ability to address and overcome both real and imagined constraints enables coachees to abandon self-limiting approaches and restrictive behaviour patterns, fostering a sense of positivity and momentum

o *Happiness and wellbeing* – furthermore this positivity and action-orientation creates a sense of greater happiness and wellbeing amongst coaches, engendering feelings of enthusiasm, hope and aspiration

o *Self-awareness and reflection* – overall CCP prompts a sense of perspective and opportunity, born of accurate self-awareness and reflection – a sense of new personal insight and discovery that enables individuals to develop a heightened sense of self-control over their destiny.

- **Organisational performance** – in addition, when applied within coaching cultures across business units and organisations, we have observed that CCP results in higher levels of engagement, productivity and discretionary effort due to improved:

  o *Leadership skills* – CCP releases the gift of accountability, enabling organisations to disseminate and manage change more effectively, unlocking higher levels of proactivity and independent action. This is important. Senior leaders cannot (due to 'distance' from subordinates and the minutiae of tasks they perform) supervise and regulate behaviour at all times. CCP fosters a sense of personal ownership and encourages individuals to independently seek their own solutions to issues and problems – a key characteristic of advanced leadership practice.

  o *Communications and relationships* – in addition, due to its emphasis upon heightening levels of personal self-knowledge, CCP improves coachees' awareness and understanding of others, leading to better relationships and communications within organisations allied to a reduction in petty politicking and conflict.

  o *Climate and culture* – the by-product of these behaviours is a more cohesive entity where people work with rather than against one another to achieve superordinate goals. It produces an environment where collaborative 'teamship' prevails, strengthening the collective capability of the organisation.

○ ***Retention and succession planning*** - as a result of this inclusive, learning, collaborative coaching climate, individuals are far more engaged and disposed to stay. Research by AaronAllen in 2016 established that engaged employees had 87% less turnover than disengaged ones (with a 78% recommendation level, three times more knowledge of customer needs and 59% higher creativity level).

But before we explore the process that leader-coaches use to RAISE awareness, BUILD accountability and REFRAME perspectives, what are the skills and characteristics required by inspirational leaders to underpin their approach?

Skills and Characteristics

It is a great benefit if the leader-coach is blessed with a fair amount of emotional intelligence in order to assist them to coach sympathetically and effectively. What do we mean by this? As Goleman pointed out in his masterful books on the subject, inspiring leaders who move people generally have *great levels of self-awareness* which in itself allows them *superior awareness and understanding of the feelings and motives of others*, resulting in healthy and *productive relationships*. Bearing this in mind, what particular skills and attributes do great leader-coaches require to coach courageously?

- **Listening and mirroring** – the first attribute they require are excellent listening and mirroring skills. On a range of levels 1-5 (where Level 1 means *planning what to say* rather than listening and Level 5 denotes actively listening to *what people mean*) it is useful if leaders are equipped with Level 5 listening skills! This will also invariably result in them being able (due to concentrated listening) to detect hidden meanings behind what people say and to interpret momentary silences and hesitations. In addition, they will be adept at mirroring their coachee's demeanour and tone in order to show empathy and respect for their feelings. That is not to say that leader-coaches abandon their aura of positivity; rather they should gauge the moment and temperature, acting with empathetic consideration and understanding.

- **Methodology and questioning** – in addition to this they will be equipped (either through explicit or tacit knowledge) with a robust methodology and appropriate battery of questions that will allow them to effectively guide conversations, help coachees resolve their issues and formulate action plans. Those that have been trained will most commonly use the TGROW model (topic, goal, reality, options and will) as their compass, although we propose our alternative BUILD-RAISE model outlined below (build rapport, understand aims, isolate issues, locate solutions and determine execution). The questions they have at their fingertips to underpin their approach should be open and non-judgemental, although effective coaches will have a range of golden reframing questions that will enable coachees to see themselves and their circumstances in a new perspective (see below).

- **Clarification and summarising** – one method by which leader-coaches can check their understanding of what the coachee has said and give them time to formulate the next pertinent question is through clarifying and summarising what has been said. Also, playing back what has been said or asking the simple question 'what do you mean by that?' is also a powerful means of reducing longwinded answers to their core. Additionally, such interventions also give the coachee time to contemplate and expand upon what they have just said.

- **Intuition and agility** – whilst we strongly urge leader-coaches to use a systematic method such as TGROW or BUILD-RAISE to advance the coachee's levels of self-awareness and accountability, effective leader-coaches (having listened deeply to what has been said) should allow their intuition to guide their questioning and probing. There will be certain windows of opportunity during the coaching interaction when the leader-coach can seize the moment to interpret hidden meanings and uncover self-justifying agendas. They should also be adept at reading *non-verbal communication* (for example, body language including facial expression and posture) to assist their interpretation of the essence of what is *really* being said and meant.

- **Mentoring** – great leader-coaches will also have another formidable weapon at their disposal, namely the ability to pass on their reflective experience to their coachees. Often the leader-coach (unlike a third-party external coach) will have the benefit of insight into the coachee's world (being familiar with the context, pressures, demands and personalities etc.). It is therefore a waste if leader-coaches miss the opportunity to pass on some of their wisdom and advice to help out coachees. However, we would make two points here. First, the whole point of the coaching process is that coachees are encouraged to solve their own issues and attain their own goals with the minimum assistance possible, in order to foster feelings of accomplishment and self-determination. Second, leader-coaches who frequently lapse into 'expert managerialism', constantly saying "when I did" or "in my experience", are likely to seem patronising and egotistical – a real turn off to the coachee! The coachee hasn't gone to the leader-coach for an extensive 'how I did it my day' lecture: (s)he expects assistance in clarifying goals, strategies in eliminating interference and credible options to move things forward!

The BUILD–RAISE Coaching Process

Great leader-coaches either develop their *own* tried and tested method of coaching, trialled and honed over a number of years coaching peers and subordinates, or they use a proxy process which they rely on as a 'route map' to help individuals resolve *career*, *development* or *performance* issues. In the previous sections we have outlined the broad skills, attributes and characteristics they require to be effective coaches, but which method do we subscribe to? Most coaching models are very similar: they start with a focus upon establishing a *purpose*, moving onto assessing *context* and the *options* available to the coachee to realise their goal, wrapping up with an agreed *plan* of action to move things forward. Over the years we have used a number of tools and techniques to coach subordinates and colleagues which – based on our experiences and observations – we have rolled into our BUILD–RAISE model of coaching (see Figure 4). This outlines a clear process for leader-coaches to follow in order to achieve the principles underlying the model which are signposted by the mnemonics RAISE and BUILD: to *raise self-awareness and build accountability* – the essential cornerstones of succesful coaching!

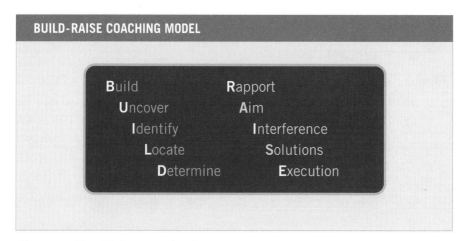

Build   Rapport
Uncover   Aim
Identify   Interference
Locate   Solutions
Determine   Execution

Figure 4 **The BUILD–RAISE Coaching Model**

This coaching model enshrines the *principle* of what the leader–coach is attempting to do (*build* and *raise* people's capability through increased accountability and self-awareness) in a sequence of memorable steps that assist them in achieving positive outcomes. These are: 'build rapport' (creating a connection, a trusting relationship that enables honest exchanges to flourish), 'uncover aim' (establishing the core purpose that the coachee is trying to fulfil), 'identify interference' (highlight the barriers and issues that are might be hampering fulfilment of the coachee's aim), 'locate solutions' (an exploration of the remedies and interventions that might enable the coachee to overcome obstacles to achieve their aim) and 'determine execution' (a viable plan of action that will enable the coachee to fulfil their aim). The sections below will go into the five elements of this model, highlighting *what* each component is seeking to achieve, *why* it is important and *how* leader-coaches go about using it (including vital tools and questions).

STEP 1 – Build Rapport

What is the leader–coach trying to achieve in STEP 1?

- **Create a trusting relationship** – the leader-coach might or might not know the coachee, but whatever their previous relationship a *climate* of trust must be established.
- **Generate chemistry** – the leader-coach and coachee must be able to 'rub along' not rub one another up the wrong way.
- **Frame realistic expectations** – at this initial stage the leader-coach needs to set expectations by outlining where the boundaries

of the relationship lie, what the responsibilities of each party are and what the coachee can expect from the sessions (i.e. *challenge with support!*).

Why?

- **Honest and open exchange** – coachees will open up and be transparent if both 'cognition-based trust' and 'affect-based trust' are evident. What are these two essential dimensions?

  - *Cognition-based trust* – is established according to how competent, reliable and dependable the coachee feels the leader–coach to be (generating feelings of confidence and respect).

  - *Affect-based trust* – is the emotional bond that develops between the coachee and leader–coach according to how much *genuine* care for their welfare the coachee thinks exists (generating feelings of attachment and gratitude).

- **Generate a topic** – the coachee might approach the first meeting with the leader–coach firmly believing that they know what issues they wish to discuss. The process of building a rapport (which can take up the entire first session) enables the coachee to relax and think more clearly about what it is they wish to achieve and/or resolve.

How do leader–coaches HELP build rapport?

- **Contracting** - first, the leader–coach and coachee need to agree parameters and boundaries:

  - *Confidentiality* – stress the confidentiality of the discussion (or agree what can and cannot be shared with the line manager)

  - *Definition of coaching* – explain what coaching *is* (challenge with support: a coachee-led process where ownership *firmly* lies with coachee etc.) and *isn't* (leader–coach owns problems, has all the answers and drives the action plan!)

  - *Scope* – agree what is 'in scope' and 'out of scope'

  - *Coaching agreement* – draw up a (formal or informal) coaching agreement detailing:

    - Values and principles by which each session will be conducted (honesty, realism, maturity, positivity, forward-looking etc.)

- Responsibilities, process and timings ('roles', timekeeping, attendance, action notes etc.)

- Expectations and outcomes (leader–coach challenge and support in exchange for coachee honesty and progression)

- **Personal interests** – they must take a genuine interest in the 'whole' person:

  - What do you do outside of work?
  - What is your passion?
  - Tell me about your family…

- **Career** – understand the coachee's career journey to date:

  - What are you most proud about in your career?
  - What motivates you?
  - Tell me about three people you most admire?
  - What do you admire about them? (This will tell the leader–coach a lot about the preferences and motivations of the coachee!)
  - What is *your* purpose in life/career? (i.e. establish discomfort with the present and a willingness to change)

- **Current role** – understand the coachee's current context, asking them to:

  - Draw a picture of yourself in your current job (a useful icebreaker that enables the leader–coach to see how their coachee perceives themselves 'in context')
  - Tell me about current stresses, strains, opportunities
  - What would be the most valuable topic to focus upon?

- **Review and discuss pre-coaching data (where available)** – such as psychometric test results (including mental toughness variables), business performance results, pre-coaching questionnaire responses, 360-degree questionnaire results etc., asking:

  - What do these results tell us about you?
  - What do they say about your strengths and weaknesses?
  - What would be the most valuable topic to focus upon?

STEP 2 – Uncover Aim

What is the leader–coach trying to facilitate in STEP 2?

- Unearth an *aim* that is:
  - *Aspirational* (i.e. stretching - will be satisfying once it's achieved)
  - *Meaningful* (i.e. matters either to the coachee or organisation)
  - *Inspirational* (i.e. passes the get 'out of bed' test)
  - *Realistic* (i.e. achievable rather than fanciful)
  - *Clear* (i.e. simply and easily expressed)
  - *Impactful* (i.e. makes a quantifiable and visible difference)
  - *Tangible* (i.e. can be measured and verified)

- Uncover the tree not the roots! Very often objectives, aims and goals are agreed by leader-coaches and coachees which address *symptoms rather than causes*. Plenty of time must be taken to set an aim which will really advance and progress the coachee. Sometimes the leader-coach must be courageous enough, having moved through the BUILD-RAISE process stages, to revisit this element and (given exploration of circumstances and resources) get the coachee to redefine their aim.

Why?

- **Essence of human spirit** – having achieved a fair degree of rapport, the process of establishing the coachee's aim runs right to the existential heart being (i.e. what are we here for and what are we trying to achieve in our lives?). Clarifying and carving out a meaningful purpose and goal is the most critical function of the leader–coach.

- **Compass and focus for discussion** – coaching sessions aren't a cosy chat - they focus on tangible issues and outcomes that are of high perceived value to the coachee. Establishing a core aim provides a reference point for subsequent discussions further on in the BUILD-RAISE process.

How do leader–coaches HELP uncover aim?

The following questions will assist leader-coaches in helping coachees to uncover their main aim:

- What do you want to achieve from this coaching session? When this session is over, what outcome would be most valuable for you? What is the most valuable thing you could take away?
- What aim do you want to achieve?
- What would you like to happen with _____?
- What do you *really* want?
- What would you like to accomplish?
- What result are you trying to achieve?
- What outcome would be ideal?
- What do you want to change?
- *Why* are you hoping to achieve this aim?
- What would the benefits be if you achieved this aim?
- If our coaching sessions are successful, what would be different for you?
- How would other people be able to tell our coaching sessions had been successful?
- What do you really want to take away from this session?
- What would you really like to do?
- Is it X or Y we need to focus upon?

STEP 3 – Identify Interference

What are leader–coaches trying to facilitate in STEP 3?

- *Isolate main barriers* – having established a viable, uplifting and measurable aim the leader-coach needs to get the coachee to list real (and imagined) impediments and derailers (that have prevented them achieving it in the past or might hold them back in the future).

- *Establish their scale* – leader-coaches should get coachees to 'rank-order' barriers in terms of their significance, to determine the magnitude of the task of overcoming them.

- *Challenge false assumptions* – by challenging and/or checking what these impediments are, the leader-coach can begin the process of challenging false assumptions and perceptions. This is particularly the case with many coachee's perception of the way others perceive what their strengths and weaknesses are. Using pre-coaching data (see above) or the Johari Window (Figure 5), leader-coaches can begin the process of uncovering the real issue: faulty assumptions about ourselves and others!

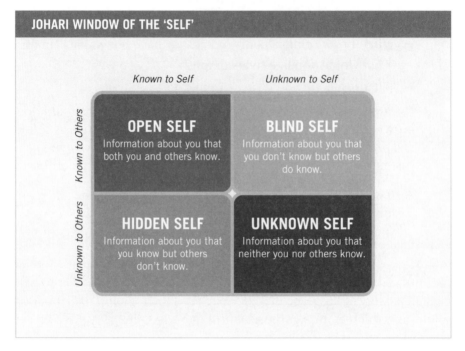

Figure 5 **The Johari Window of the Self**

Why?

- **Potential – interference = positive outcomes** – the major reason why leader–coaches need to identify the nature and extent of interference is because – as this equation from Miles Downey's masterful book *Effective Coaching* highlights – the isolation and elimination of interference releases people's potential, resulting in more positive outcomes.

- **Self-limiting attitudes and behaviours** – very often we are our own worst enemies in preventing ourselves from reaching our aims, objectives and goals. Using the Johari window (see Figure 5) increases coachee awareness of their 'blind self' but if we were to caricature what really holds coachees back (as we've found over years of coaching and observation) we would highlight:

- o *Excessive ego within men* – a need to be *perceived* as outperforming their peer group and having a position of high social standing within 'the pack' which bolsters their sense of identity and self-worth… which in itself causes stress, anxiety and sub-optimal behaviours!

- o *Lack of self-confidence within women* – a sense that (in spite of past achievements) what they have done - or plan to do - is *never* good enough… which in itself causes stress, anxiety and sub-optimal behaviours!

- **Create sense of perspective and new insights** – in addition, coachees might be labouring under false misconceptions as to the real barriers facing them at the workplace. Great leader–coaches help cast new light on the *real* sources and true extent of the obstacles coachees face in attempting to realise their principal aim.

How do leader–coaches HELP identify interference?

This stage of the process needs to be taken very slowly. Why? Because interference needs to be described in rich detail. The coachee needs time to think and reflect on what might be hindering them. The leader–coach must make sure at this stage that the coachee does not jump to ill-founded solutions (which is the next stage of the model). Questions that will aid the process at this stage include:

- What is happening now (what, who, when and how often)? What is the effect or result of this?
- Have you already taken any steps towards your aim?
- How would you describe what you did?
- Where are you now in relation to your aim?
- On a scale of one to ten, where are you?
- What has contributed to your success so far?
- What progress have you made so far?
- What is working well right now?
- What is required of you?
- Why haven't you reached that aim already (issues)?
- What do you think is stopping you?
- What do you think was really happening?

- Do you know other people who have achieved that aim?
- What did you learn from _____?
- What have you already tried?
- How could you turn this around this time?
- What could you do better this time?
- If you asked _____, what would they say about you?
- On a scale of one to ten, how severe/serious/urgent is the situation?
- If someone said/did that to you, what would you think/feel/do?
- What is the present situation in more detail?
- What and how great is your concern about it?
- Who is affected by this issue other than you?
- How much control do you personally have over the outcome?
- Who else has some control over it and how much?
- What action steps have you taken on it so far?
- What has stopped you from doing more?
- What obstacles will need to be overcome on the way?
- What resources do you already have? (Skill, time, enthusiasm, money, support, etc.)
- What is really the issue here, the nub of the issue or the bottom line?

STEP 4 – Locate Solutions

What is the leader–coach trying to facilitate in STEP 4?

- **Surface remedies** – having established the main sources of interference that are hindering progress towards the coachee's aim, the leader-coach will help them surface a range of viable and *plausible* options that will neutralise them. Often these remedies will not be earth-shatteringly innovative, but having spent a great deal of time considering what the real barriers are, they are more likely to be solutions that fit these obstacles.

- **Highlight enablers** – in addition, the leader-coach will help the coachee identify a range of core resources that the coachee will require to eliminate interference, namely: developing better skills and capabilities, creating wider networks, drawing upon existing contacts, feeding off past experiences, identifying and utilising key strengths etc.

Why?

- **Move things forward** – often coachees have been completely immobilised by what, to them, had seemed to be insurmountable blockages preventing them from realising core goals. What the leader-coach is doing is helping the coachee to *envision* a credible way of moving things forward. This is not to say that the coachee - following the session - will be fully equipped to eradicate all interference in one go. Often, what the leader-coach is doing is providing 'the spark' - encouraging the first of a series of small steps in a journey that will ultimately help the coachee achieve their ambition.

- **Provide hope, confidence and unlock energy** – having been paralysed by a sense of helplessness, the discovery of a range of solutions to seemingly overwhelming odds will, in all likelihood, re-energise the coachee, provoking renewed feelings of hope and confidence that they can reach their desired destination. However, the leader-coach must caution the coachee that any solution is unlikely to be a complete panacea to (sometimes) complex and ambiguous issues. (S)he must ensure that the coachee understands the scale of their task, which can be broken down into bite-sized chunks by the action plan that they will draw up and agree at the end of the session (see Step 5, 'Determine Execution', below).

How does the leader–coach HELP locate solutions?

Fundamentally, what the leader-coach is attempting to do in this stage is to reframe the coachee's perspective, opening them up to new ways of seeing, viewing and tackling the obstacles they face by using:

- **Pictorials** – using models and frameworks which help coachees discover new ways of tackling problems.

- **Mentoring** – intervening with mentoring advice and expertise on how certain issues (based on the leader-coach's prior experience) can be tackled.

- **Reframing questions** – locating solutions and resources through the use of compliments, exceptions to the problem, prioritisation (do more of what works, do less of what doesn't work!), encouraging small steps through scaling and the use of possibility language. Many of these types of questions are outlined below and are addressed in more detail in the 'Reframing Perspectives' section at the end of this chapter.

- What are your potential solutions? What could you do? If you could do anything, what would you do? If you could only apply one solution that would add the most value what would it be? What would be the results of this action?
- What do you think you need to do next?
- What could be your first step?
- What do you think you need to do to get a better result (or get closer to your aim)?
- What else could you do?
- Who else might be able to help?
- What would happen if you did nothing?
- What has worked for you already? How could you do more of that?
- What would happen if you did that?
- What is the hardest/most challenging part of that for you?
- What advice would you give to a friend about that?
- What would you gain/lose by doing/saying that?
- If someone did/said that to you, what do you think would happen?
- What's the best/worst thing about that particular solution?
- Which solution do you feel ready to act on?
- How have you tackled this, or a similar situation, before?
- What could you do differently?
- Who do you know who has encountered a similar situation?
- If anything was possible, what would you do?
- What personal strengths do you bring to this?
- How confident are you on a scale of 1–10 that you can do this?
- What else?

STEP 5 – Determine Execution

What is the leader–coach trying to facilitate in STEP 5?

- **Clear action plan** – having uncovered a clear aim, identified potential interference and located viable solutions, the leader-coach must now get the coachee to commit to a clear plan of action with timescales and deliverables. During the coaching session (at least in formal circumstances) the leader-coach will have made notes or a sketched a 'fishbone diagram' detailing how the coachee has arrived at this point. It is now beholden upon the coachee, with prompting and probing from the leader-coach, to commit to a minimum of (in our experience) at least *three* measurable and quantifiable action points.

- **Support and resources** – in addition to what the coachee commits to do, they need to specify how they will do it – including the enabling resources they require for success (e.g. time, money, line-manager or stakeholder support). At this juncture, the leader-coach can also offer support, potentially drawing upon their own resources and contacts to help the coachee fulfil their overarching aim (without the coachee losing accountability for its ultimate achievement).

- **Follow-up and evaluation** – having agreed a written plan of action, dates for follow up and analysis of its progress are necessary so that the coachee has clear milestones in place. This follow up can take place during the next coaching session or 'down the wire'. The important point is that the coachee knows that they will be held to account and judged accordingly at some point in the near future in order to motivate them to act swiftly (in spite of the myriad of other things they have to do in their day jobs!).

Why?

- **Progress** – at its heart, coaching is all about making progress. The leader-coach's role is to provide courageous challenge with support, raising the coachee's level of self-awareness and building their accountability to move things forwards. Coachees can experience elation and exuberance in the coaching session. However, where a coachee is insufficiently mentally, physically and practically prepared, these feelings can immediately dissipate outside the coaching bubble, 'when the rubber hits the road'. The leader-coach must guard against this. 'Feel good' coaching sessions are a waste of time unless they are translated into tangible progress.

- **Momentum** – leader-coaches have enough to do themselves without signing up to a mountain of post-session support. The leader-coach must guard against 'carrying' or getting too close to the coachee at this stage. But in order to ensure the plan gathers momentum, a few catch-up calls or emails from the leader-coach to check on progress in-between coaching sessions can help animate the process.

How does the leader–coach HELP determine execution?

In order to mobilise positive, proactive and productive behaviour, the leader-coach clearly needs to get the coachee to map out a number of clear steps and check for *absolute commitment* to an agreed plan of action. The questions below are designed to help in this process:

- How are you going to go about executing the plan? What will you do and when?
- What do you think you need to do right now?
- Tell me how you're going to do that.
- How will you know when you have done it?
- Is there anything else you can do?
- On a scale of one to ten, what is the likelihood of your plan succeeding?
- What would it take to make it a ten?
- What obstacles are getting in the way of success?
- What roadblocks do you expect and what will require planning?
- What resources can help you?
- Is there anything missing?
- What one small step will you take now?
- When are you going to start?
- How will you know you have been successful?
- What support do you need to get that done?
- What will happen (or, what is the cost) of you *not* doing this?
- What do you need from me/others to help you achieve this?
- What are three actions you can take that would make sense this week?
- On a scale of one to ten, how committed are you to doing it?

- What would it take to make it a ten?
- Is this an efficient use of your time?
- How committed are you to actually doing this?
- How can you keep track of your success?
- What are all the different ways in which you could approach this issue?
- Make a list of all the alternatives, large or small, complete and partial solutions.
- What else could you do?
- What would you do if you could start again with a clean sheet, with a new team?
- What are the advantages and disadvantages?
- Which would give the best result?
- Which of these solutions appeals to you most or feels best to you?
- Which would give you the most satisfaction?

REFRAMING AND MAGIC QUESTIONS

We referred to the use of reframing questions in Step 4 'Locate Solutions', but a number of these questions are scattered among the ones we outlined in all stages of the BUILD–RAISE coaching process. However, given their importance – their capacity to jolt and change coachees by generating revelatory perspectives and new ways of thinking and seeing things – further consideration of the specific types and genres of these questions is useful here. More precise definitions of these type and an illustration of how they can be used can only be of help to leader–coaches that truly wish to shift feelings, attitudes, perceptions and behaviours.

Reframing Perspectives by Using and Leveraging

- **Compliment-based questions:**

  Flattering concerns to move forwards, for example:
  Coachee: "It's far *too costly* to implement."
  Leader-coach: "I'm *impressed that you are cost conscious*! How can you make the solution less expensive?"

- **Exception-based questions:**

  Highlighting previous successes to advance, for example:
  Coachee:"I find that *person really difficult* to work with".
  Leader–coach:"It sounds difficult... Tell about the *times or a situation in which you have worked well* together."

- **Possibility-based questions:**

  Envisioning options to nudge things on, for example:
  Coachee:"I really *can't relate to that individual.*"
  Leader–coach:"So, to date you really haven't been able to communicate in order to develop a relationship... I wonder *what might assist in forging good communications?*"

- **Resistance statements:**

  Reducing the problem to get started, for example:
  Coachee:"There is *no way I could get all of that done* given the pressure I am under!"
  Leader–coach:"That's understandable! *What elements could you do?*"

- **Relationally-based questions:**

  Third-party perspective to stimulate, for example:
  Coachee:"I can't do it!"
  Leader–coach:"Tell me *who would be surprised* to hear you say that?"
  ("What else would your boss see?", "Who else would notice a difference?", "If you had a friend in a similar situation, what would you advise?")

- **Miracle-based questions:**

  Envisioning a positive future to change mindset, for example:
  Leader–coach:"If you awoke tomorrow to *find this problem gone*, how would you feel? What would your life be like?"
  ("Imagine you are performing more effectively – what are you actually doing differently?")

- **Scaling questions:**

  A point of reference for measuring change over time, for example:
  Leader–coach:"Rank the *importance of this aim on a scale*

from 1 to 10. Now rate your actual performance against this objective. Where do you want it to be?"

- **Comparison-based questions:**

  Use context to generate proper perspective, for example:
  Leader–coach: "When you say this is a major issue, can you be more specific: is it *more/less* than *who/what?*"

- **Coping-based questions:**

  Surface coachee resilience to generate hope, for example:
  Leader–coach: "*What do you do* to keep going?" ("Tell me about the reserves you currently draw upon to cope with your situation.")

- **Mindfulness-based questions:**

  Promote self-awareness, leading to more solution-focused options for improvement, for example:
  Leader–coach: "*What else* did you see/feel/do?"

- **Metaphor-based questions:**

  Help coachee to think differently/creatively, for example:
  Leader–coach: "Paint a picture for me – what are you actually trying to achieve?"
  ("If you were to write a book on this what would it say? What character would you play?")

- **Problem-free talk:**

  Where the leader–coach creates a judgement-free zone and conversations about (seemingly) irrelevant life experiences help illuminate coachee strengths and resources to move things forward.

CASE STUDY 19 – **THE LEADER-COACHING SESSION** BY CHRIS EDGER

Here, in a fictional scenario based on true events, the HRD (the COACH) of a major multi-branded leisure corporation, holds a coaching session with the Chief Operating Officer (the COACHEE) utilising the BUILD–RAISE process, interspersed with reframing questions.

(Build Rapport)
COACH: "Great to see you. How's the family? How are the kids?"
COACHEE: "Growing up fast..." [Discussion on family ensues.]
COACH: "In our last session we set a clear goal – for you to *strengthen your team* by appointing Claire to run Brand X and move John – the incumbent – to a central support role. This was to be achieved within six weeks and we discussed strategies as to how you might achieve this. Can you update me on progress?"
COACHEE: "Since that meeting I've met with both John and then Claire. John has agreed to move to Central for career-development purposes: I think he was relieved really – he's been heading the brand for four years – and accepts that he has taken it as far as he can. I've agreed with Simon (CEO) and Alison (Marketing Director) that he takes up the vacant Marketing Services Director position – he'll add a lot there. Claire is really excited about taking over the brand and we've organised handover dates etcetera."
COACH: "So everybody's happy and – overall you've strengthened your organisation. Your worries about how John might react were unfounded! Well handled! Now... what topic would you like to discuss this time? Anything causing you concern or slowing you down? What would you like to achieve in this session?"

(Understand Aim)
COACHEE: "Obviously, growing the business – I don't think we're going fast enough! But I always feel that way... Something specific that's really causing me concern at the moment is my relationship with the new Chairman. I don't think he rates me. And that's not great for my career: the Chairman thinking I'm an idiot!"
COACH: "So what do you want to accomplish?"
COACHEE: "I suppose I want to change his perception of me."
COACH: "If our coaching sessions on this issue were successful, what would be different for you?"

COACHEE: "I would have a plan going forwards, whereby I could get the new Chairman to have confidence in me and forge a good relationship."

(Identify Interference)
COACH: "If you had to rate your relationship with your Chairman on a scale of 1–10, where is it now and where would you like it to be?"
COACHEE: "Currently I'd rate it at a 2/10. It would be great if it were 8/10! Obviously, we're never going to be bosom buddies."
COACH: "OK. Describe the present situation in more detail... What really is the issue here, the nub of the issue or the bottom line?"
COACHEE: "Got off on the wrong foot... First time out in the business he started asking silly questions and then making naïve comments about how we could do things better... He suggested we rename one of our implant concepts... So I started questioning him on his view about upcoming legislation (he clearly didn't have a clue about it!) and I think that offended him... I have no chemistry with him... He doesn't understand the business... Since then he's sort of dismissed or ignored me when he's been in meetings."
COACH: "Describe to me what you felt when you'd heard he'd been appointed. How did you rate his appointment on a scale of 1–10?"
COACHEE: "I thought: who is this guy? Is this the best we can do? I rated him no better than a 2!"
COACH: "So, just to clarify – you rated his appointment as a '2' and you think he rates you as a '2'! If somebody you knew was listening to this conversation what would they say to you?"
COACHEE: "They'd say – typical! You don't rate this guy – even though he's more powerful than you and you've let it show. He's sensed your attitude and now you're paying the price."
COACH: "You clearly don't rate him: that's what you feel. But tell me three things about him that you have a sneaking admiration for..."
COACHEE: "One, he has built some good businesses in other sectors. Two, he is energetic. Three, he does have very good manners towards our colleagues."
COACH: "So, he does have some redeeming features. Tell me, if you woke up tomorrow and this problem was gone – how would you feel?"
COACHEE: "Relieved. I really don't need this stress at the moment."

(Locate Solutions)
COACH: "So, what are your potential solutions? If you were advising someone else who was in exactly the same position – what would you advise?"

COACHEE: "Perhaps – now I think about it – I need to change *my* attitude towards him. Perhaps I have been a little immature. He has picked up on the fact that I don't rate him and he has responded in kind. This situation isn't going to benefit either of us – certainly not me! So I really need to get closer to him."

COACH: "In the past when you've had a rocky relationship with somebody who matters, how have you mended fences?"

COACHEE: "I've learnt to take more time understanding their anxieties and viewpoint."

COACH: "So what anxieties and concerns does your new Chairman have, do you think? If you were in his shoes what would you feel?"

COACHEE: "I suppose he feels his reputation is on the line by taking this job. He wants to show some progress quickly: he wants to grow the business..."

(Determine Execution)

COACH: "If I understand you right, that's what you said *your* overarching goal was at the top of this discussion! So you are both aligned in that! So tell me what you are going to do next to mend relations? What one small step can you take *now*?"

COACHEE: "Funnily enough, I am out with him next week for the day. So I can use my time with him to forge a better relationship."

COACH: "How do you move your relationship towards an 8/10 during that day out?"

COACHEE: "First – as I've said – change my attitude towards him. Second, ask him about his concerns, anxieties and objectives – try to understand where he is coming from. Three, try and allay some of those fears by showing him what we are doing to grow the business. Set things up on the day so that he goes away with more knowledge and confidence about me and the business."

COACH: "So to clarify: your plan is to a) change your attitude towards him, b) listen and understand where he is coming from and c) demonstrate alignment and competence. Is there anything I can do to help?"

COACHEE: "Not at the moment, thanks. But, I've written those three things down in my log. Do you mind if I reflect on them and give you a quick ring before I go out into the business with him next week?"

COACH: "Not at all! I've also made notes. Report back to me on how you believe you have fared in moving his perception of you from a '2'. Next time we will reflect on what happened and consider further actions you can take to strengthen your relationship with him."

Chapter Summary

This chapter focused upon one-to-one leader–coaching that compliments the practices that we argued inspirational leaders apply in some of the 'ten moments of emotional truth' we outlined in the previous chapter. Courageous coaching is an essential tool for the inspirational leader, enabling them – having positively mobilised team members at a *collective* level – to *independently* address their psychological needs, *facilitating progress and advancement*. It promotes self-awareness and accountability amongst the recipients, which is essential in environments where the inspirational leader does not have the answers to every problem, fostering a climate of personal ownership, creativity and organisational agility. But if we were to summarise the key attributes, skills and practices of great leader–coaches – what would they be? Here are our 26 key insights into great leader–coach practice:

GREAT LEADER–COACHES

- **Courageously challenge** – coaching is not a 'soft' conversation (or a chat or whining session): IT IS CHALLENGE WITH SUPPORT! Good leader-coaches are 'loving boots'.

- **Use open questions** – they always use what, where and how probing questions - they never use why?! Why? Because coaching sessions are focused upon advancement and progress rather than self-justification or wasteful introspection.

- **Exhibit curiosity, humility and respect** – great leader-coaches are coachee focused: they do not use the coaching sessions as a personal grandstanding opportunity.

- **Control the process *not* content** – the leader-coach expertly concentrates upon guiding the process and does not exclusively influence the content (which should be predominantly coachee-led).

- **Increase coachee receptiveness** – leader-coaches will actively seek to gain coachee buy-in to the process by

---

establishing high levels of rapport and confidence as a result of their demeanour, approach and expertise (the coachee *must* have the willingness and capacity to learn and willingness to change).

- **Let the coachee find solutions** – the leader-coach is a facilitator, a process owner, a prober and a challenger - (s)he is focused upon promoting awareness and accountability. (S)he is not the party that finds solutions - this responsibility must lie with the coachee, in order to ensure buy-in and ownership.

- **Focus on behavioural change** – in order for coachees to achieve personal, career, developmental or performance goals, leader-coaches address underlying attitudes, motivation and future behaviours.

- **Actively listen and ask** – leader-coaches have deep listening skills (they listen and don't just *hear*). *They are present*!

- **Ask for permission to mentor** – at various junctures, leader-coaches will ask the coachee for permission to make observations based on their prior expertise and wisdom.

- **Use silence** – leader-coaches don't attempt to fill silence: they use it judiciously to allow contemplation and thinking to occur.

- **Watch body language** – it is estimated by experts that 70 per cent of our messages are conveyed through our body language (facial expression, gestures, bodily disposition etc.). Great leader-coaches are masters at interpreting these non-verbal signals.

- **Suspend their judgement** – great leader-coaches are not there to scrutinise and judge. Rather they non-judgementally guide the process with one singular aim: to assist in *advancement*.

- **Use their intuition** – leader–coaches use their intuition (as well as their grounded knowledge and expertise) to guide the coaching conversation to a purposeful and uplifting conclusion.

- **Choose an appropriate time and place** – leader–coaches will ensure that their sessions are unencumbered by interruptions or distractions. That is not to say that all coaching sessions need to be formal set-piece engagements. Some of the most effective coaching interventions are short and sharp, held down-the-wire or in a quiet space at the workplace.

- **Know when the coaching cycle has ended** – great leader–coaches accurately judge the end of conversation cycle, i.e. when the coachee has achieved what they originally set out to solve or the relationship has run its course.

- **Positively focus on *future* improvement** – leader–coaches are aware that coachees will (inevitably) have preconceived ideas as to what will happen in the future based on past experiences. In particular, negative experiences (seared into the memory) are likely to colour their mindset and behaviour. Effective leader–coaches always *start with the future* but also help coachees to review the past in a more positive context (focusing on what was done well and achieved) in order to focus coachees on the art of the possible, going forwards.

- **Use the inner resources of the coachee** – in order to construct positive forward momentum, great leader–coaches are adept at helping identifying the strengths and personal resources (i.e. networks) of the coachee to move things ahead. Often, coachees underestimate the resources (both personal and organisational) that they have at their disposal to eliminate interference and achieve their aims.

- **Challenge faulty self-perceptions** – often the greatest barriers to progress do not lie around the coachee but within them (through misguided perceptions and limiting self-beliefs). Great leader-coaches REFRAME PERSPECTIVES by provoking insight into, and acknowledgement of, this hindrance. Great leader-coaches recognise that, until they complete this task, the coachee will be unable to move off 'first base'.

- **Evoke positive imagery through stories** – in order to disrupt previous patterns and assumptions, leader-coaches will (at the right time) ask coachees to recall times when they have prevailed in order to trigger *positive visual imagery* and thought patterns which will be the necessary precondition for forward advancement. At appropriate times (when adopting a mentoring capacity) leader-coaches will draw upon their own metaphors and stories to reframe the feelings, views and perspectives of the coachee.

- **Create a trusting relationship** – one immutable law which must not be transgressed at any time is that of coachee confidentiality. That is to say that leader-coaches cannot (unless they are given explicit permission) disclose any intimate details of the discussions they have had during sessions that are designated for pure coaching purposes. The absence of such an ethically binding arrangement will result in a lack of trust, limiting levels of honesty and disclosure.

- **Are flexible during the coaching process** – although leader-coaches will follow a method which is intended to take their coachee to the desired outcome, their management of the process will not necessarily follow a sequential or linear pattern. Why? Because the reality is that revelations and discoveries 'in process' will, in all likelihood, lead to the redefinition of aims and means of execution.

- **Keep a professional distance** – great leader-coaches don't get emotionally engaged with the coachee. They are able to separate their own emotions from both the subject and the coachee, in order to maintain a focus on process and achieve positive outcomes. This is not to suggest they are cold and dispassionate. Far from it. Their line of questioning, tone of voice and body language radiate empathy, compassion, curiosity and understanding. But this is underscored by steely professionalism and a firm resolve to help the coachee locate solutions to their problems.

- **Have a growth mindset** – great leader-coaches have a growth mindset, namely: the belief that the world is full of possibility and potential *and* that they have the capacity to transition coachees out of a fixed mindset (a negative perception that they are powerless to change either themselves and or the circumstances that surround them).

- **Ensure follow through** – acknowledging the fact that their coaching sessions do not take place in isolation from the real world - where coachees will have choices and distractions - great leader-coaches ensure that agreed actions are followed through. This is achieved by agreeing a course of action and then checking progress in subsequent coaching encounters. Whilst leader-coaches might offer some support in terms of resource, time and networks, they do not attempt to fix problems themselves: accountability firmly lies with the coachee to *own and fix it*!

- **Don't act like a therapist or counsellor** – whilst leader-coaches help coachees to discover their 'blind selves' (that which is unknown to themselves but seen by others), (s)he keeps clear of exploring the 'hidden self' (that which is unknown both to the leader-coach and the coachee). Coaching focuses on personal progress not regressive therapeutic diagnosis (that might uncover childhood trauma having a connection with psychological issues). Where leader-coaches find that their coachees have deep psychological problems, they should recommend that the coachee seeks professional medical help.

- **Create coaching-style cultures** – ultimately, leader-coaches create a spark within organisations, a vibe that holds that coaching is a useful hard (rather than soft) developmental tool that can improve relationships, wellbeing and performance. Those that have been coached (and have found it useful) are trained to coach others. Communities of practice thrive where co-coaching and supervision networks support a vibrant coaching culture focussed upon advancement, creativity and progress.

'Your emotions are the slaves to your thoughts, and you are the slave to your emotions...'

Elizabeth Gilbert

EMOTION

Underpinning this entire book is our explicit belief that our concept of eMOTION (the mobilisation of positive feelings) is crucial for inspirational leaders: creating super-performing teams and individuals. But it would be remiss of us if we did not formally address the meaning of 'emotion' itself. As the word from which our 'eMOTION' derives, we will consider why it is important and what science has to say about it. We could have outlined this at the beginning of the book but we wanted a 'fast start', concentrating the reader's attention (whilst we still had it) on the essential purpose, principles and practices of inspirational leaders. But if you've made it this far, here are some further insights and justification for our endeavour!

Definition

Let's firstly deal with how 'emotion' is actually defined and what it means. The Anglo-Saxon word 'emotion' is derived from the latin 'emoveo' – which means 'to move, stir up or agitate' – and the French 'emouvir' ('to excite'). This combination leads to its classic definition: "a *strong feeling* deriving from one's circumstances, mood or relationships with others". Our preferred definition – echoed in the title of this book – also includes the notion of action: "moving people into action through *shifting their feelings*".

The concept of emotion as a strong force in human behaviour can be traced back to ancient Greek playwrights, Shakespearean plays and the Romantic movement. Here 'passions' and 'humours' were described as strong irrational impulses that drove humans into action – often with disastrous consequences! In the mid-nineteenth century, emotion began to be incorporated into scientific enquiry, through works such as Darwin's *The Expressions of the Emotions in Man and Animals* in which he made the claim that emotions were evolutionary 'inherited reflexes' stemming from a need to survive (stimulating 'fight or flight' feelings) and reproduce (satisfying pleasure and procreation feelings). At the turn of the twentieth century, psychologists such as Freud and Jung observed - though intensive single case-study research - that emotions had a complex connection with the mind, through which they could be consciously or unconsciously repressed, built up or unleashed.

But how are emotions scoped and defined today? Scientific and general insights will be looked at in more detail in this book later but, put simply, psychologists have made three major observations about emotions:

- **Emotional pleasure and levels of arousal vary in strength –** psychologists generally plot emotions along two continuums (pleasant–unpleasant and high–low arousal). Within these continuums, psychologists have plotted a number of 'sensory states' that humans experience according to mood and circumstance. However, generally - in keeping with the 'pleasure principle' - psychologists have located a limited number of anchor feelings.

- **Emotion incorporates seven basic feelings –** as stated, psychologists have identified a select number of 'prime', 'basic' or anchor feelings that humans can experience. Although they can't agree on the exact number and nature of these feelings, the seven basic emotions that show up in studies time and time again include: *anger, sadness, fear, surprise, disgust, contempt* and *happiness*. Different expressions of these prime feelings manifest themselves in different forms. For instance, happiness being expressed in secondary expressions of joy, delight and excitement.

- **Emotion incorporates three stages –** the expression of emotion is processed through three fundamental stages: *physiological > feeling > behaviour*. That is to say the brain is stimulated by physiological circumstances, triggering high/low pleasant/ unpleasant feelings that lead to automatic behavioural responses (that are either suppressed or exhibited). Unlike rational cognitive thoughts that can take time to process (humans having only the capacity to think in 'unitary' terms, i.e. one thought at a time), emotional responses are instinctual and therefore far quicker, translating feelings into behaviour much faster.

The implications of these findings for leaders are pretty obvious. Humans are equipped with highly sophisticated emotional reflexes that enable them to sense and quickly react to opportunity or threat. Leaders have an opportunity to summon up positive responses/actions through arousing, animating, mobilising and optimising pleasurable feelings. Or - indeed - reframing and shifting negative feelings into positive ones! But why is this so important now, more than ever?

Why Is Emotion Important Now?

We believe there is an urgent need for leaders to understand and drive positive emotion amongst their teams at this time more than at any other. Why? Here are our four reasons:

- **The emoji phenomenon** – in the past, customers and employees have been asked by organisations how they felt over a range of issues. This is usually done by surveys asking them to express satisfaction or dissatisfaction on a 1–10 scale (where 1 means very unsatisfied). This will change. The emoji revolution, allowing people to pick from a range of 'faces' to represent how they feel, will give people far more licence to convey their real convictions. Whereas they might have given a low score in the past to signal their dissatisfaction, they will now pick an emoji image that they feel more powerfully conveys their true feelings: possibly opting for angry, disgusted or frustrated expressions! Indeed, the fact that the emoji revolution has occurred and caught on is a powerful testament to the need for humans to express their true feelings to one another in more evocative, imaginative and impactful ways. A 2016 report on macro trends in the UK food service sector written by the consultancy Heidrick and Struggles warned food service leaders that "a negative emoji can destroy your brand". Brand leaders will be forced to respond to such feedback quickly in order to transform negative 'angry' emoji feedback into positive 'smiley' emoji advocacy. By the same token, organisations with sophisticated real-time employee feedback systems will be able to enable staff to convey their true feelings through emojis. A revolution will occur in the way that leaders analyse and shift the emotional climate within their teams and company into 'positive emoji territory'.

- **Need to counteract depersonalising technology** – many years ago the academic John Nasebit called for organisations to be "high tech but high touch" as they sprang forward into the digital revolution (echoing the longstanding Japanese concept of 'Jikota' which exhorts organisations to implement 'technology with a human face'). What he was insinuating was that although, in order to maintain competitiveness, organisations needed to keep up with technological trends, they should still pay heed to the 'human factor'. Humans are social, sentient animals who (generally) seek the company of others. On the one hand, digitalisation has increased and opened up further channels for human interaction and self-expression. But studies show that, far from replacing the social and mental health benefits of one-to-one human interaction, digitalisation has caused greater feelings of loneliness, resentment, anger and detachment. Particularly when such technology is displayed in service industry contexts. In the service sector, digital mechanisation has fuelled feelings amongst customers that companies, through cutting back on the 'personal touch', have begun to lose their humanity. Staff in 'lean service machines' act like worker drones, operating under tight surveillance, using equipment designed to optimise productivity and efficiency rather than enhancing the customer experience. It has never been more important for leaders to use technology as a means rather than an end in itself. Technology will never replace the basic human need for some degree of customer intimacy within service interactions.

- **Need to roll back transactional leadership** – in his famous book on leadership, Warren Bennis characterised two types of leader: the transactional and the transformational. The typical transactional leader (rather like Douglas McGregor's Theory X manager) intrinsically believes that most workers are untrustworthy and lazy, needing strong authoritarian 'carrot and stick' management to stimulate desired behaviours. The transformational leader, on the other hand (bearing a close resemblance to McGregor's Theory Y manager), has a more benign view of human nature, believing people to be fundamentally trustworthy and willing: open and susceptible to operating under looser, more participative supervision. The reality today is that many leaders peddle the rhetoric of transformation ('our greatest asset are our staff') whilst meting out a reality of harsh transactional practice. Why? Here are some of the reasons why leaders reject the concept of emotionally connecting with their people and teams:

○ ***It is too difficult*** – spending time and energy tapping into and harnessing people's positive emotions requires a high degree of time and effort. As Chris Moore (former CEO of Domino's Pizza) remarked: "EQ (emotional quotient) is more important than IQ for service business leaders, but few are willing to wholeheartedly commit themselves to leading in this way – because it's too sticky!" Some leaders have risen to the top due to their IQ and lack EQ skills (and fail to surround themselves with peers who might compensate for this blind spot). Others cannot be bothered to make the effort, falling back instead on command-and-control practices as a means to 'get things done'.

○ ***Emotion is taboo*** – furthermore, in the atmosphere of 'hard-arsed' boardrooms where discussion of hard financial outputs rather than of soft people inputs is preferred, the notion that board members should discuss the feelings of employees (other than giving a cursory glance at the annual employee survey) would be regarded as laughable – a sign of weakness on the part of any individual that tried to push this agenda! This sets the cultural dynamic within which many companies operate, creating a trickledown effect of greater focus upon the numbers rather than the people. Rationalism rather than charisma is the order of the day in many companies. This is an approach that flies in the face of the fact that humans respond more readily to inspiring imagery than to dry fact.

○ ***They don't get the service–profit connection*** – in addition, many leaders fail to accept (or understand) the well-established linkage between a motivated workforce, satisfied customers and positive sales outcomes. They fail to understand that, particularly in service businesses, where staff are required to requite customers' desires for *speed, quality and warmth*, employees need to feel cared for before they show the same level of appreciation and concern for customers. They reject this equation, misguidedly believing staff to be expendable cogs in a machine that – because of the way 'they' have designed it – will continue to perform well, with or without staff that care.

○ ***Race to the bottom*** – within the prevailing business

environment where technological innovation is overturning outmoded business models, leaders turn to reducing costs on the labour line as a means of sustaining short-term profit. In service businesses, employment costs can account for anything up to 35 per cent of overall operating costs in some operations, so it stands to reason that reducing costs in this area will have the largest (and quickest) payback in terms of reducing overhead. Whilst such approaches might be needed from time to time to 'rebase' the business, the fact remains that leaders often embark on wave after wave of staff overhead reductions that spread disillusion, fear and uncertainty amongst their teams, which has a knock-on effect on customer perceptions of service. They fail to communicate their reasons for making these reductions, when they will end and how such actions will ultimately contribute to growing the business. In short, they fail to engender feelings of *hope* that things will ultimately get better!

The net outcome of this transactional leader approach is feelings of fear, resentment and discontent amongst employees. Over the past eight years, intensive mental toughness tests applied to over 800 middle managers from some of the UK's largest retail, leisure and hospitality companies at Professor Chris Edger's Academy of Multi-Unit Leadership revealed that their greatest 'resilience deficiency' correlated to low levels of 'emotional control'. That is to say, managers negatively responded to emotional control statements such as: "I generally look on the bright side of life"; "When I am upset or annoyed, I usually let others know"; "Even when under considerable pressure I usually remain calm"; "I generally hide my emotion from others"; "When I am feeling tired I find it difficult to get going"; and "I can usually control my nervousness". Further probing as to the causes of negative responses to these questions showed that these managers felt they were the victims of transactional rather than transformational leadership regimes, where the efficiency paradigm was valued far more highly than effectiveness.

But ultimately, such leadership approaches are counterproductive and unsustainable. People are crying out for inspirational leadership! In a general sense, the issues that face Western civilisation today – terrorist threats, global warming, economic 'rebalancing' (a redrawing of the unsustainably generous post-World War Two social-welfare contract) – demand strong, purposeful leadership. Bland bureaucratic greyness will not wash – the Trump effect in the US and the Farage effect in the UK in 2016 have highlighted how citizens in Western societies are searching for more charismatic solutions to the problems they face. At a corporate level, as Daniel Pink pointed out in his powerful treatise on contemporary leadership, people are crying out for purpose, autonomy and mastery. Transactional leadership approaches will not deliver this. Inspirational leadership that seeks to connect emotionally with the needs, feelings and aspirations of people during these disorientating times is what people crave.

• **Need to reframe the engagement agenda** – a huge amount of university research and corporate effort has been targeted at understanding and creating 'employee engagement'. What we would argue is that, over time, the mechanics and principles underpinning employee engagement have fallen into disrepute. It has become undone through being over-hyped, badly researched and imprecisely applied. In reality, EOS (employee opinion surveys) are often mechanistically applied by managers who merely seek to get the scores up year on year because it forms part of their scorecard! Also, do these surveys capture how people really feel and – most importantly – how they are going to act? No. In short, the engagement agenda has been captured and held hostage by HR professionals who are (generally) no more qualified to understand human behaviour than their colleagues in Finance. Engagement surveys that confirm that people feel contented do not measure their intention to expend discretionary effort. They do not capture levels of passion and arousal for the cause. They fail to calibrate or harness the true emotional temperature of the organisation. Furthermore, as annual surveys, they are merely a snapshot of opinion at one moment in time and can be purposefully manipulated by the managers who commission them (for example, by being sent out just after bonus time or prior to unannounced 'organisational design' exercises). We believe that such tools and mechanisms are now outdated and redundant. As we pointed out above, the emoji revolution will reframe the way in which people will be able to express their *true inner feelings*. Also, digital technology will enable leaders to feel the pulse of their organisation far more frequently than ever before, enabling them to respond to feelings and concerns more quickly than in the past.

So, the requirement for leadership that harnesses people's positive emotions is more pressing than ever! But what is the competitive advantage on offer for those that purposefully and energetically seek to do this?

The Competitive Advantage of Emotion

In a world of technological impersonality, lazy and deficient leadership practice and meaningless engagement data, clear opportunities exist for companies that focus upon animating positive feelings amongst their employees. Earlier on in the book, we outlined what best practice looks like, highlighting the 'Ten Moments of Emotional Truth' that inspirational leaders concentrate their efforts upon in order to mobilise their teams and organisations. But broadly, what competitive advantages does focusing on optimising positive emotional states amongst employees provide to organisations that do it? We believe the advantages lie in four main areas:

- **Quality** – having employees that are emotionally attuned to the purpose (and values) of the organisation and the needs of its customers will lead to a quality product delivery. As Henry Ford said, "quality means doing it right when nobody is looking!" Employees who care about their organisation, their jobs and customers will be more inclined to provide the perfect product for customers. Nowhere is this more important than in dispersed multi-unit service chains where local operators – unlike their fixed-site manufacturing counterparts – cannot be constantly scrutinised for delivering operational excellence. In effect, teams in these environments are self-regulating, executing the product blueprint to the highest standard without direct supervision from the centre. Getting it right first time, every time or quickly remedying problems through creative solutions makes service personnel feel good, with customers perceiving quality levels to be high – thereby increasing their propensity to advocate to friends, family and/or social media and to revisit.

- **Experience** – but this is not just about quality and consistency. Employees with positive emotional mindsets will not only execute the product well, they are also more likely to deliver superior 'front of mind', exceptional customer experiences. What do we mean by this? Service businesses, in particular, comprise a combination of tangible and intangible elements. Whilst *good* businesses attend to tangible product quality well, *great* businesses address intangible elements such as service delivery in a superior way to their direct competitors. How do they do this? By employing service personalities who are happy in their work, enjoy the company of their colleagues and delight in creating memorable experiences for their guests. Great service businesses employ people who 'get' the fact that, in effect, during their interactions with customers, they are 'on stage' being scrutinised for warmth, congeniality, proactivity and personality. Businesses that employ and motivate staff to provide positive experiences that become seared on the consciousnesses of their guests are highly likely to gain competitive advantage in a business landscape generally populated by companies that provide mediocre or sub-standard experiences!

- **Reputation** – those organisations that deliver quality and memorable guest experiences inevitably garner a good reputation. But more than that, they achieve deep customer intimacy and *trust*-based relationships with their customers. And trust lies at the heart of reputation: a faithful belief by consumers that their chosen brand will repeatedly deliver upon its promise and (more often than not) exceed expectations. This is something that is constantly augmented and strengthened through the multiple interactions that customers have with happy, positive, empowered employees who make it their mission constantly to burnish the reputation of their employer.

- **Sustainability** – the net result of quality, experience and reputation is that the brand achieves sustainability. Inevitably, in order to be successful on a long-term basis, the business must evolve with the times. In addition, leaders must ensure that they maintain a balance between the main elements of the proposition (product, environment, service and price), guarding against any deadly combinations that might degrade consumer perceptions (for instance, product quality being compromised by perceptions of over-pricing). However, businesses that stimulate high levels of 'lifetime customer value' ensure the long-term viability and sustainability of the firm. The link between this sustainability and creative, proactive team members who are alert to the needs of the business constantly to refresh, whilst delivering its core proposition, cannot be overstated. Again, having staff that are emotionally attached and 'in for the duration' lends competitive advantage in a corporate world where brands can rise and fall in increasingly short timeframes.

Understanding the Science of Emotions

There are thousands of books that discuss engagement and motivation but many of them lack any scientific explanation of the ways in which humans are pre-programmed to react to their context and circumstances. Many offer trite psychological generalisations on the way in which people respond to situations and predicaments, with little empirical back-up. This is unsatisfactory. Over the past couple of centuries, scientists have investigated the way in which human brains process emotional responses, and their findings and insights are highly relevant for this book. Overall, we would select five insights on the way in which the brain processes emotion as being particularly significant:

- **Primal instincts stimulate the brain to act** – it was Darwin who first established that emotions served a basic evolutionary purpose. Based on his observations of genetic mutation, he argued that in order for a species to continue, it needed to survive and transfer on its genetic coding. Hence, he believed that *primal emotions* like *fear* shielded humans from threats so they could pass on their genes, triggering fight-or-flight responses that primed the body to defend itself or run away from danger. On the other hand, he argued, emotions like *love* and *lust* furnished humans with the desire to reproduce. In both circumstances, the brain assumes the function of evaluating a stimulus - such as a car that is about to run you over or an attractive poster of a supermodel - and creating an emotional response (fear or lust). In short, the brain is programmed to act in terms of how it can best respond to circumstances in order to *survive* and *reproduce*, using primal emotions as the trigger to activate physical responses.

- **'Brain chemicals' stimulate emotions** – the brain is a complex network that unscrambles vast quantities of information every nanosecond. The brain's information-processing network employs *neurons* - receptor cells that receive and transfer signals around the brain - and these neurons despatch signals through *neurotransmitters*, 'brain chemicals', which some neurons release and receive. The two most commonly studied neurotransmitters relating to emotion are:

○ ***Dopamine*** – this is a brain chemical released when pleasure is experienced, either directly or as part of a reward-learning process. Thus, when humans do something good, they are rewarded with dopamine which stimulates feelings of happiness. Such feelings teach your brain to crave it constantly, leading to habitual behaviours that go in search of a dopamine high!

○ ***Serotonin*** – this brain chemical is related to memory and learning. Scientists believe that serotonin helps to regenerate brain cells, a factor that may contribute to easing depression. Any imbalance in serotonin levels can result in increases in anger, anxiety and panic.

Any problems in the way the brain receives and processes these chemicals can have a significant effect on human emotions. For instance, when humans experience something rewarding or pleasurable, the area of the brain that processes that information interacts with the brain chemical dopamine. If the brain is incapable of receiving dopamine normally, the result is that humans are less happy or sad. Also, studies of people with major depressive conditions have shown that they have fewer serotonin receptors in their brains to regenerate brain cells and ease anxiety.

• **Different emotions are processed by different parts of the brain** – the brain is made up of many different components that simultaneously process the information it receives. What are they?

○ ***Limbic system*** – often called the 'emotional brain', this is the main part of the brain responsible for processing emotions.

○ ***Amygdala*** – as part of the limbic system, the amygdala processes the emotional intensity of stimuli and is the principal part of the brain associated with fear 'fight or flight' responses.

○ ***Hypothalamus*** – this regulates how humans respond to emotions, for instance, causing the heart rate and blood pressure to rise and breathing to quicken.

○ ***Hippocampus*** – this transforms short-term into long-term memory and also helps humans retrieve stored memory. Memories inform humans how they respond to their circumstances, incorporating instinctive 'learned' responses.

It therefore stands to reason that because separate elements of the brain process varying emotions in different ways, damage to any part might dramatically change moods and emotions.

- **Emotions are kept in check by the brain's hemispheres** – the brain is divided into two equal-sized hemispheres which work together to keep humans functioning, each taking responsibility for processing different types of information. The *left* side of your brain thinks more *rationally*, interpreting the literal meaning of things, while the *right* side thinks in a more *abstract* manner, picking up imagery and symbolism. As the two sides process information differently, they need to work together coherently in order to keep human emotions in balance. So as the *right* brain identifies negative emotions (such as fear and anger), it alerts the *left* brain, which decides what to do by coming to a logical decision about how to respond. This symbiosis between the two hemispheres is crucial. For instance, in the absence of left-brain functions, the right brain would be overrun with negative emotions and would fail to identify how to respond to them.

- **Emotions are driven by memories and habit** – given the role of the brain's hippocampus in generating and storing short- and long-term memories, it is unsurprising that scientists have established that recalling negative memories generates bad mood and feelings, whilst thinking about positive memories can place humans in a good mood. Psychological studies back this up. They have proven (through techniques such as cognitive behavioural therapy) that memory recall can be used to shift the moods of depressives, because recalling positive memories causes the brain to release dopamine, creating a craving to recall these positive memories time and again to temper any negativity. In addition, memories of past experiences influence how humans instinctively respond to situations. If an individual has had a near-death experience on an aircraft flight, they may experience intense feelings of fear on their next aircraft journey (as the intensity of the previous experience will heighten their level of emotional intensity).

Key Insights

In addition to the insights on emotion already provided within this chapter, what are the *key* findings, insights and observations relating to emotion?

Emotions are the most significant motivator of human actions – in essence they enable humans to survive, reproduce, create social bonds and act morally. It has been established that emotional responses are nearly ten times faster than 'unitary' cognitive thought processes.

There are over four hundred words for different emotions – *positive* descriptors include: happiness, affection, awe, calm, contentment, courage, curiosity, delight, desire, ecstasy, empathy, enjoyment, euphoria, excitement, gratitude, happiness, hope, interest, joy, love, passion, pleasure, pride, satisfaction, surprise, trust, warmth and wonder. *Negative* descriptors include: anger, anxiety, anguish, apathy, contempt, despair, disappointment, disgust, dismay, dread, exasperation, fear, frustration, hatred, hunger, humiliation, impatience, indignation, irritation, panic, paranoia, rage, sadness, shame, shock, suspicion, terror, uncertainty and worry.

Facial expressions convey emotions – studies have established that facial expressions betray emotion 99 per cent of the time and that, in addition, if humans adjust their facial expression to reflect an emotion, they actually begin to feel that emotion. Indeed, a human can use their forty-three facial muscles to make over ten thousand facial expressions to express a wide variety of subtle emotions! Interestingly, emotions and facial responses have been found to be universal (even if their 'triggers' are less so). The facial expressions of Londoners and Eskimos are the same when experiencing the same emotions (especially joy and disgust!).

Body language often reveals emotion – like facial expressions, non-verbal body language betrays emotions. For instance, a person standing with their legs wide apart, their arms upon hips and elbows turned outward is giving off an assertive territorial behaviour display (signalling aggression). Also, touching the nose indicates a human is hiding something (portraying fear of discovery).

Smell affects emotions – smell can have a powerful and immediate effect upon emotions. Why? While visual, auditory and tactile senses are processed by our various brain sensors, smells have a *direct* path through the olfactory cortex (behind the nose) *straight* to the amygdala within the brain, where emotions originate. Also, scent-based memories tend to take hold in the brain in ways that memories associated with other senses do not. This is why certain smells (such as those associated with childhood) can provoke such deep emotional responses, even if the recipients are not aware of the reason. Scent-based memories are created and stored in infancy – preceding intellectual development – and retain their strength of recall for far longer than other types of memories.

Colours can affect emotional responses – whilst not every human experiences the same emotion in response to a particular colour, most people find reds and oranges stimulating and greens and blues (primal colours of the sky and jungle) restful. In contrast, grey, brown, black and white tend to have a dulling effect.

Emotions are contagious – humans can spread their negative or positive emotions as those around them 'imitate' or are emotionally 'infected' by their feelings. Interestingly, negative or unpleasant emotions are *more* contagious than neutral or positive emotions!

Humans can simultaneously experience contrary emotions – humans can feel 'mixed' emotions at times, simultaneously feeling a complex mixture of both happiness and sadness (when watching a weepy film, for instance).

Emotional expression is instilled at infancy – men *and* women experience the same amount of emotion, but women tend to physically exhibit them more. Why? Studies have concluded that mothers are less tolerant of crying in boys, inferring that the way emotions are expressed by adults is instilled during their infancy.

Emotions vary in length according to mood – emotions can last from less than a second up to several minutes (although sad emotions tend to affect humans for longer than positive ones). However, moods last much longer than emotions – from minutes up to several days – and affect how humans experience emotions. For instance, if humans are in an irritable mood, they tend to experience anger more rapidly than usual.

Humans can cultivate and shift their emotions – humans have the capacity, through brain functions, to switch their attention from an emotion, to interpret it differently or even to change the meaning of it (thus modifying their reaction to it). This can be achieved with help from third-party intervention (such as a counsellor, coach or therapist) or through heightened self-awareness. The earlier humans can recognise an emotion (such as fear, anger or disgust), the more equipped they are to deal with it.

Emotional intelligence is linked to success – studies have shown that 85 per cent of an individual's financial success is related to their personality and ability to communicate and lead. Only 15 per cent is directly related to IQ.

Negative emotions can be beneficial – Anglo-American self-improvement 'pop psychology' argues that positive thinking is critical to humans in achieving their goals and finding happiness. Negative thinking is regarded as somewhat detrimental to the pursuit of self-fulfilment. This is, however, somewhat simplistic! Recent research suggests that a capacity to process negative emotions successfully is the key to good mental health. Negative thoughts help humans understand and assess their experiences: attempting to suppress them can end up having the opposite of the desired effect. Furthermore, the celebrated psychologist Martin Seligman has suggested that excessive optimism may "keep us from seeing reality with the necessary clarity". This is not to suggest that lingering negativism is good for humans; rather, it's the ability to process, compartmentalise and deal with negative feelings that is believed to result in a more positive outlook.

Controlled exposure to fear increases resilience – if humans are given controlled exposure to something that they inherently fear, they will become more resilient to its perceived effects. By conditioning the mind to recalibrate and reprocess the experience, their perception of danger can be lessened through gradual accomplishment (the positive outcome of which can be stored in the memory). Humans can thus learn to confront and overcome irrational (and sometimes rational!) fear responses in the future.

Conclusion
eMOTION and Inspirational Leadership

Having outlined our research and insights into what underpins truly inspirational leadership, we would like to end this book by reflecting on what we believe to be the core purpose, practices and qualities of these leaders. But before we do, let us remind ourselves what our central argument is: *that capturing and harnessing eMOTION must be the holy grail for any leader wishing to engage and inspire employees and/or partners to achieve extraordinary tasks which they would otherwise have thought impossible*. It is this one quintessential ability that differentiates effective leaders from inspirational ones. Inspirational leaders have the ability to *transform* the way that their teams and people feel: *shifting* negativity into positivity, *touching* hearts as well as minds, *mobilising* behaviours that result in truly extraordinary outcomes. Why is this so effective? Simple. Humans are sensory beasts: activating the senses results in quicker and more profound outcomes than dry logic or rationality. Inspirational leaders *move* teams and people by *reframing* the way they feel about themselves and the world around them. They reframe people's perspectives and expectations, *uplifting* their spirits, inculcating a glass half full rather than a glass half empty mentality. The net result is that the teams and organisations they lead are far more agile, responsive, creative and productive.

Their Purpose and Principles

But what is the starting point for inspirational leaders? What is the essential foundation for their success? We would argue that it is this: inspirational leaders are able to articulate clearly *why* they are in business, *what* the true purpose of their organisation is and *what* their guiding principles are in a compelling and attractive manner. In short, they have a **noble cause** supplemented by a central belief system that energises and inspires those around them. Neither of us has ever met any successful individual entrepreneur who started out with a spreadsheet and a business plan rather than a desire to be a pioneer or to do something before or better than anyone else! Likewise, the more time we have devoted to studying successful businesses, companies and organisations, the more we have concluded that profit is not the cause that drives them, but merely the by-product of their endeavour. They are driven by a constancy of purpose or, as they see it, a noble cause, accompanied by clearly defined principles which guide them always to 'do the right thing'. People are attracted (not recruited) to these organisations because they identify and subscribe to their noble cause as if it were a religion or calling. Joining and remaining are not rational decisions based just on remuneration and reward but *emotional commitments* to becoming a disciple of the noble cause. Witness great organisations through history that have harnessed the *emotional connection* and commitment of their disciples: religious orders, medical practitioners, charities, caring organisations and military forces. In industry, organisations that we have cited in this book - such as the John Lewis Partnership, Ritz Carlton, Pret a Manger, Apple, Nando's and Southwest Airlines - stand out as having articulated a noble cause backed up by strong guiding principles.

This is supported by the case studies in this book. Several inspirational leaders were able to articulate the noble cause they defined for their organisation, backed up by firmly held principles. Here are a few select examples:

- Justin King, CEO, Sainsbury's (2004-14)[On his noble cause:] ...the idea of **'Making Sainsbury's Great Again'** really came from listening to how our customers and colleagues in the business were *feeling* at that time. Customers *felt* that "this was once a great place to shop where I *loved* doing my weekly grocery shop and I'd really *love* to come back and do that again". And our colleagues felt that they "used to be *proud* to work here. I *loved* working here. I'd tell my friends that I was here and I would envisage the rest of my career here. But now I hope nobody asks me where I work because I don't want to admit it". So the 'Making Sainsbury's Great Again' was all about "we're going to take the business back to that *feeling* for you...".[On his guiding principles:] As you'll gather from my view of the world, *as long as you're focused on customers and colleagues*, then that's almost inevitably going to reap rewards for the corporation and therefore serve the best interests of the shareholders!

- Simon Vincent, EMEA President, Hilton (2006-present)[On his noble cause:] [To create] brands that are *loved* - it is first and foremost about our brands. Customers [must] love our brands. You only have to look at the customer feedback that we get and the REVPAR premiums that our brands enjoy over and above the competition. Each one of our individual brands enjoys a REVPAR premium over the completion in their respective customer segment.[On his guiding principles:] Hospitality and proactivity – we are all about hospitality. 'We are hospitality. We are Hilton!' And that's what we aim to do. We aim to serve our guests and hopefully they'll come back and stay with us over a lifetime. I think our culture is absolutely defined through the word 'hospitality' but I think we also operate to very high levels of integrity. *We have a real sense of urgency in our business now, in terms of getting things done. One of our values is 'Now!': living in the moment, making things happen, driving performance.*

- James Spragg, COO, Casual Dining Group (MD Café Rouge, 2014–16)[On his noble cause:] We had to get back to basics. This brand started life as an *authentic all-day French bistro*: warmly serving classic, *authentic French food done really well*… We were a 'heritage' rather than a 'cool fashion' brand and we had to go after and delight our core customers… This brand need to be *nurtured, protected* and *loved* again…[On his guiding principles:] …in addition, we had to put some emotion back into the brand by getting our people to believe and *care* about what they were doing… the board and I were visible and *present* in the business: people could see that we *cared* as much as they did about the business and if we *cared* more about our customers than our competitors – we won!

What stands out from these accounts – and the many others in this book – is the importance of connecting with people (both staff and customers) at an emotional level, crafting a noble cause and supporting principles that make people *feel* inspired and motivated. To this extent the accounts from inspirational leaders that illuminate this book constantly reinforce and validate our position. That is to say, that inspirational leaders galvanise and mobilise people though emotional rather than rational connection. They intuitively understand the importance of making people feel that they are part of something worthwhile, important and good. That they too can make their mark by achieving something of significance. That their working lives have a *deeper* existential purpose and meaning.

Their Practices

This noble purpose and its accompanying principles shape mindsets, feelings and desired behaviours. But this ethos must be supported by a number of practices during the employment cycle that mobilise super-performing teams. To this end, we have designed a model that clearly illustrates how – during the 'Ten Moments of Emotional Truth' of the cycle – inspirational leaders mobilise their teams and people through our concept of eMOTION, showing their specific practices and approaches that generate positive feelings and behaviours. This sits at the heart of this book, so it is essential that we briefly reprise both the model and its various components.

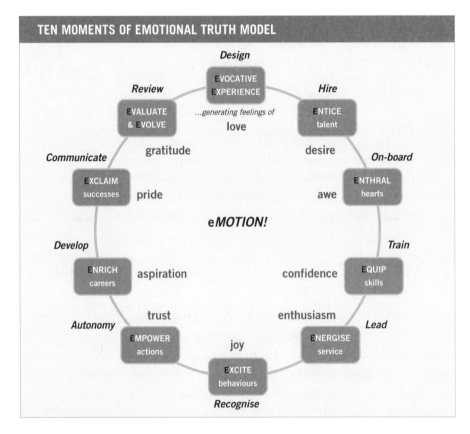

Figure 6 **The Ten Moments of Emotional Truth Model**

#1 EVOCATIVE EXPERIENCE – Design (generating LOVE): the start
point for inspirational leaders is designing a product or service
experience that – rather than being regarded with ***ambivalence*** –
sears itself onto the hearts of all participants and recipients, creating
deep-seated levels of ***love***, attraction and attachment. How? As
stated above, by standing for something good, creating a warm
personality and providing distinctive and generous benefits to *all* that
interact with it. Inspirational leaders understand that if customers
love their product and service, staff will love it too!

#2 ENTICE TALENT – Hire (generating DESIRE): inspirational leaders
need great service personalities to deliver a great product but many
will be embedded elsewhere – what they need to do is overcome
feelings of ***caution***, creating a great hunger, appetite and ***desire*** to
join their 'elite team'. How? By promising worthwhile work, taking an
'uncorporate' approach to hiring (by putting their people's stories
upfront) and by winning over opinion formers (parents, peers and
careers advisors) as well as potential applicants. Declaring that they
are not hiring for 'what you have done in the past but what you are
capable of achieving in the future' is a message that inspirational
leaders deploy to create desire.

#3 ENTHRAL HEARTS AND MINDS – Onboard (generating AWE):
once onboard, inspirational leaders negate any ***scepticism***,
exceeding newbies' pre-set expectations, engendering feelings of
amazement, wonder and ***awe***. How? By offering a warm welcome *on
the first minute of the first day*, providing a thorough immersion
programme (including heart-warming stories, legends, symbols and
icons) and pairing them up with buddies who help and uplift them.

#4 EQUIP SKILLS – Train (generating CONFIDENCE): at the same
time, newbies are prevented from feeling exposed and ***vulnerable*** by
being furnished with the wherewithal and resources to do the job,
adding courage, conviction and ***confidence*** to their endeavours.
How? By clearly establishing key principles ('your job is to make
customers happy!') backed up with technical training for quality,
behavioural training for emotional intelligence (including non-verbal
communication and 'mood' management) and cognitive training for
problem solving and planning.

#5 ENERGISE SERVICE – Lead (generating ENTHUSIASM): frontline
leaders make it their primary objective to win the 'shift battle'
through galvanising their teams, creating a sense of verve, zeal and

enthusiasm to service customer needs rather than letting them fall prey to feelings of **apathy** and disillusionment. How? By making sure units are 'set up for success' pre-session, setting the dynamic tone by modelling desired behaviours out on the floor, adjusting their leadership styles according to individual requirements (task-led for 'don't knows' and delegation-led for 'can do's'), rapid decision making in the heat of battle and 'getting people's backs' when unwarranted criticism arises.

#6 EXCITE BEHAVIOURS – Recognise (generating JOY): inspirational leaders know that recognition has a profound effect on behaviours, animating and enlivening people, creating surprise and **joy** – rather than **exasperation** at being taken for granted. How? By rewarding service behaviours through transparent and timely incentives, giving pay increments for the acquisition of extra skills and competencies, providing staff (and particularly managers) with some 'skin in the game', always celebrating success together, and what we call 'planned spontaneity', meaning instantly rewarding and recognising people when you have caught them doing it right!

#7 EMPOWER ACTIONS – Autonomy (generating TRUST): given their teams' requirement to service multiple occasions, needs and 'touch points', inspirational leaders know that they should outsource a degree of delegated authority and decision making to the frontline. This not only generates higher customer satisfaction but also makes staff less **frustrated**, making them feel more **trusting**, valued and in control. How? By providing clear guidance on 'no go', 'check than go' and 'go' parameters, allowing signature acts of self-expression, actively encouraging feedback on improvements (which are listened to and acted upon quickly) and – in extreme circumstances – allowing people to apply patch ups and workarounds to ensure business continuity.

#8 ENRICH CAREERS – Develop (generating HOPE): inspirational leaders will also make sure that maximum opportunity is given to both 'ambitious' and 'pillar' staff (who often **despair** at being overlooked) to enrich their careers through development paths and programmes that meet their **hope** and *aspirations* for progression or career sustainability. How? By providing clear progression paths, accredited and certified professional development programmes (that mean something to the outside world), effective career transition mechanisms that reduce transition shock for those switching jobs (upwards or sideways) and targeted mentoring/on-the-job coaching that helps individuals to grow and/or progress.

#9 EXCLAIM SUCCESSES – Communicate (generating PRIDE): at the same time, inspirational leaders ensure that they overcome **cynicism** by having open, honest and vibrant communications that enhance feelings of belonging, achievement and **pride**. How? By focussing content around key messages (with a fixation upon progress and growth), cascaded through channels (e.g. face to face communication, digital 'pulse' briefings and 'closed' social-media circuits) that are quick, *visual* and impactful.

#10 EVALUATE AND EVOLVE – Review (generating GRATITUDE): finally, inspirational leaders must have performance review systems in place to quell feelings of **apprehension** by enabling people to know how they are performing and where they stand. These will (largely) promote feelings of relief and **gratitude** amongst staff, *most* of whom want to be perceived as doing a good job. It is also an opportunity for inspirational leaders to have courageous conversations with people who are not cutting it, suggesting that there are great opportunities for them elsewhere! How? Through regular formal performance appraisals and coaching, plus – most importantly – informal ad hoc discussions which reduce levels of fear and anxiety amongst self-critical high performers that they aren't doing as well as they should. In addition, inspirational leaders should keep evolving the organisation's proposition, operations and capability in order to keep ahead of the game. This is something that some will feel uncomfortable about and resist – but many will welcome and feel grateful for!

In addition to implementing and pursuing practices that generate feelings of love, desire, awe, confidence, enthusiasm, joy, trust, aspiration, pride and gratitude, we also highlighted the role that inspirational leaders play on a one-to-one basis through their roles as Courageous Coaches. To this end, our BUILD–RAISE model of coaching provides a framework for leaders to help advance and progress their people by challenging them, thus raising their levels of self-awareness and accountability. For, whilst inspirational leaders clearly require a range of emotional interventions that work at a collective level, they also require ones that work at a more intimate, one-to-one level too, to *reframe* perspectives and subtly *nudge* attitudes, mindsets and behaviours.

Their Qualities

So inspirational leaders have the ability to articulate a noble cause, backed up with authentic principles and practices that *mobilise positive feelings and behaviours*. But what personal qualities do they have? We have argued in this book that they have four main qualities: inspirational leaders are **spiritual** (exhibiting a *heartfelt purpose* and *cast-iron values*), **holistic** (characterised by high levels of *tacit knowledge* and an *inclusive mentality*), **optimistic** (underpinned by a *positive mood* and *growth mindset*) and **proactive** (exemplified by the capacity to be '*black box thinkers*' and have a *simplicity of focus*). We have also referred to the requirement for inspirational leaders to have higher than average levels of emotional intelligence (EI) in order to practice eMOTION. Surveying the evidence of this book and reflecting on the encounters with the inspirational leaders we interviewed and countless others we have met during the course of our careers in business and academic research, what elements of EI would we draw attention to as being particularly important?

- **Self-awareness and mental toughness** – the combination of knowing oneself and exercising personal control through high levels of mental toughness is an important feature of the inspirational leader. Due to the workload and associated pressures/stresses of the role, such leaders need to acquire a degree of self-knowledge and discipline with regards to how they react to certain situations, demonstrating a fair amount of manners and grace under immense provocation (as illustrated by Jens Hofma, the CEO of Pizza Hut, in Case Study 12). It is our belief that inspirational leaders demonstrate the following behaviours with regards to self-awareness and mental toughness: *honest reflection, a desire for improvement* and *an ability to listen to feedback* (promoting self-awareness), *adaptiveness to different challenges* and *circumstances, emotional self-control under pressure, a balanced view of success and failure, a focus on 'controlling the controllables'* and *confidence in one's own abilities* (fostering mental toughness).

- **Awareness of others and reciprocity** – self-awareness will undoubtedly help the inspirational leader – through the process of understanding 'self' – to read the motives/desires of their followers. This informs them as to which practices/approaches they should adopt with individuals/teams to shift feelings and mobilise positivity: inducing reciprocity and indebtedness to get things done (as Simon

Longbottom, CEO of Stonegate, highlights in Case Study 15). However, in order to shape and control emotions, we believe inspirational leaders display the following attributes: *empathy* (authentic questioning and listening skills), *processing* (ability to read/interpret the motives and feelings of others) and *fit* (the ability to apply the right interventions that generate positive feelings and behaviours).

- **Relationship and conflict management** – in addition to self-awareness and awareness of others, inspirational leaders (like Peter Long, Chairman of TUI, in Case Study 2 and Simon Vincent, President of Hilton EMEA, in Case Study 4) are adept at fostering and maintaining good relationships across their team and organisation. Inspirational leaders are able to deal with ambiguity, understanding that most organisations are riven by competing interests and that it is their role to minimise conflict by creating 'win-win' solutions that everyone can buy into. Sometimes they will have to 'bring the hammer down' or 'bash heads together', but generally they will seek to drive consensus and alignment through more subtle and sophisticated means. They create advocates and strong coalitions who will put aside personal enmities and competing interests in furtherance of the common good.

Are these essential characteristics of EI developed through nature or nurture? We would argue that the answer is both! Although some modicum of EI requires implantation early in life (through social interaction with family, friends and peers), it can be improved and augmented later on through good role models and personal development (psychometric testing, 360-degree feedback, learning logs and targeted coaching and mentoring). But what we essentially believe is this: eMOTION is fundamentally a belief system that leaders either buy into or ignore. They either intuitively understand the importance of neutralising negative feelings in order to nurture positive feelings amongst their staff or they don't! As we argued in the previous chapter, most leaders are far more inclined to focus on outputs rather than inputs – putting profit before people. That is why, for those who choose to practice eMOTION, it is a distinctive form of competitive advantage.

Final Comments

So where does all this lead us? It is a belief held by both the authors and the contributors to this book that practising eMOTION reaps dividends for business leaders. *Mobilising super-performing teams and individuals by attending to how they feel – shifting negative mindsets, thoughts and behaviours into positive territory – is **the critical skill of the inspirational leader!*** We would offer three final thoughts. First, there are many who will deride some of the concepts and insights within this book. They will label our obsession with *transforming feelings* as 'soft' and 'woolly'. They are wrong. eMOTION advances a plausible framework with tangible outcomes. We have gone beyond most books of this genre to address how business leaders can make people feel better and, as a result, produce better outcomes for themselves, their teams and organisations. Ruling by promoting a climate of fear paralyses and inhibits people, creating stress and serious mental health issues. Leading by inspiring people – making them *feel good* and *moving* them to achieve great things – encourages creativity, productivity and high levels of engagement. Second – listen in! – eMOTION is not costly but the returns can be startling. Paying attention to how your people feel and ensuring that you have the right purpose, principles and practices in place to foster eMOTION is inexpensive. It requires a leap of faith more than an extortionate investment in time and money. Third, it is the only way you can run a business that is sustainable in the long term. *Businesses without feelings have no heart. Businesses with no heart go out of business.*

Sources and Further Reading

Autry, J. (2001) *The Servant Leader.* NY: Three Rivers Press.

Barrett, L. (2017) *How Emotions Are Made: The Secret Life of the Brain.* London: Macmillan.

Bass, B.M., and Bass, R. (2008) *The Bass Handbook of Leadership: Theory, Research, and Managerial Applications* (4th edition). NY: Free Press.

Bennett, N., Wise, C., Woods, P.A., and Harvey, J.A. (2003) *Distributed Leadership.* Nottingham: National College of School Leadership.

Blake, R.R., and Mouton, J.S. (1964) *The Managerial Grid: The Key to Leadership Excellence.* Houston: Gulf Publishing.

Burns, J.M. (1978) *Leadership.* NY: Harper & Row.

Cook, S. (2008) *The Essential Guide to Employee Engagement: Better Business Performance through Staff Satisfaction.* London: Kogan Page.

de Vries, M.F., Korotov, K.R., and Florent-Treacy, E. (2007) *Coach or Couch: The Psychology of Making Better Leaders.* Paris: INSEAD Business Press.

Drucker, P.F. (1955) *The Practice of Management.* London: Pan Books.

Dweck, C. (2017) *Mindset: Changing the Way You Think to Fulfil Your Potential.* New York: Ballantine Books.

Edger, C. (2012) *Effective Multi-Unit Leadership – Local Leadership in Multi-Site Situations* (1st hardback edition). London: Routledge.

_____. (2013) *International Multi-Unit Leadership – Developing Local Leaders in Multi-Site Operations.* London: Routledge.

_____. (2014) *Professional Area Management – Leading at a Distance in Multi-Unit Enterprises* (1st edition). Oxford: Libri.

_____. (2015) *Professional Area Management – Leading at a Distance in Multi-Unit Enterprises* (2nd revised edition). Oxford: Libri.

_____. (2016) *Retail Area Management – Strategic and Local Models for Growth.* Oxford: Libri.

_____. (2016) *Effective Multi-Unit Leadership – Local Leadership in Multi-Site Situations* (2nd paperback edition). London: Routledge.

Edger, C., and Emmerson, A. (2015) *Franchising – How Both Sides Can Win.* Oxford: Libri.

Edger, C., and Hughes, T. (2016) *Effective Brand Leadership – Be Different. Stay Different. Or Perish!* Oxford: Libri.

Evans, D. (2003) *Emotion: A Very Short Introduction.* Oxford: OUP.

Fayol, H. (1916) Administration industrielle et generale. *Bulletin de la Societe de l'Industrie Minerale*, 10, 5–164.

Fieberg, K. (1998) *Nuts! Southwest Airline's Crazy Recipe for Business and Personal Success.* New York: Broadway Books.

Fiedler, F.E. (1967) *A Theory of Leadership Effectiveness.* NY: McGraw-Hill.

Gallup Organisation (2012) *The Relationship Between Engagement at Work and Organisational Outcomes.* Omaha, Nebraska.

George, B., Sims, P., McLean, A.N., and Meyer, D. (2007) Discovering Your Authentic Leadership. *Harvard Business Review.* February, 129–38.

Goleman, D. (1996) *Emotional Intelligence.* NY: Bloomsbury.

_____. (1998) *Working with Emotional Intelligence.* NY: Bantam Books.

Hersey, P., and Blanchard, K.H. (1993) *Management of Organizational Behavior: Utilizing Human Resources* (6th edition). NY: Prentice-Hall.

Heskett, J., Jones, T., Loveman, G., Sasser, W., and Schlesinger, L. (1994) Putting the Service Profit Chain to Work. *Harvard Business Review.* March–April, 164–74.

Holbeche, L., and Matthews, G. (2012) *Engaged: Unleashing Your Organisation's Potential Through Employee Engagement.* San Francisco: Jossey-Bass.

Kahneman, D. (2012) *Thinking, Fast and Slow.* London: Penguin.

Kerr, J. (2013) *Legacy: 15 Lessons in Leadership.* London: Constable & Robinson.

Kotter, J.P. (1982) What Effective General Managers Really Do. *Harvard Business Review,* 60 (6), 156–62

_____. (1996) *Leading Change.* Harvard Business Review Press.

KPMG/IPSOS Retail Think Tank (2014) *How will Demographic Trends Affect the Retail Sector?* London.

Kroc, R. (1997) *Grinding It Out.* Chicago: St Martin's.

Mayer, J.D., Salovey, P., Caruso, D.R., and Sitarenios, G. (2001) Emotional Intelligence as Standard Intelligence. *Emotion* 1, 232–42.

_____. (2003) Measuring Emotional Intelligence with the MSCEIT V2.0 Edition. *Emotion,* 3, 97–105.

Meyer, D. (2010) *Setting the Table: The Transforming Power of Hospitality in Business.* New York: Harper.

Michelli, J. (2008) *The New Gold Standard: 5 Leadership Principles for Creating a Legendary Customer Experience Courtesy of the Ritz-Carlton Hotel Company.* New York: McGraw-Hill.

_____. (2011) *The Zappos Experience: 5 Principles to Inspire, Engage and WOW.* New York: McGraw-Hill.

Mintzberg, H. (2009) *Managing.* London: Pearson.

Murphy, M. (2012) *Hiring for Attitude: Research and Tools to Skyrocket your Success Rate.* Leadership IQ Paper, Washington DC.

Peters, S. (2012) *The Chimp Paradox: The Mind Management Programme to Help You Achieve Success, Confidence and Happiness.* London: Vermilion.

Pink, D. (2011) *The Surprising Truth About What Motivates Us.* Edinburgh: Canongate.

Reichheld, F. (2003) One Number You Need To Grow. *Harvard Business Review.* December.

Schultz, H. (2008) *Pour Your Heart into It: How Starbucks Built a Company One Cup at Time.* New York: Hyperion.

Seligman, M. (2011) *Flourish.* Australia: William Heinemann.

Skinner, B.F. (1976) *About Behaviorism.* New York: Vintage Bodis.

Smith, T. (2016) *The Book of Human Emotions: An Encyclopaedia of Feeling from Anger to Wanderlust*. London: Profile Books.

Syed, M. (2016) *Black Box Thinking: Marginal Gains and the Secrets of High Performance*. London: John Murray.

Timpson, J. (2010) *Upside Down Management*. Chichester: John Wiley.

_____. (2015) *High Street Heroes: The Story of British Retail in 50 People*. London: Icon Books.

Walker, M. (2014) *Best Served Cold: The Rise, Fall and Rise Again of Iceland Foods*. London: Icon Books.

Whitmore, J. (2009) *Coaching for Performance: The Principles and Practices of Coaching and Leadership*. London: Nicholas Brealey.

Wilkinson, M. (2013) *The Ten Principles Behind Great Customer Experiences*. Harlow: FT Publishing.

Yukl, G. (2006) *Leadership in Organizations* (6th edition). Upper Saddle River, NJ: Prentice Hall.

Index